To

Best wishes

J. Henry

JOHN HENRY'S
············· *Guide to* ·············

BACKCOUNTRY
ADVENTURE
in
CATHEDRAL PARK

The essential guide to backcountry camping, alpine hiking and mountain goat viewing in Cathedral Lakes Provincial Park B.C.

 FriesenPress

One Printers Way
Altona, MB R0G 0B0
Canada

www.friesenpress.com

ISBN
978-1-03-917720-8 (Hardcover)
978-1-03-917719-2 (Paperback)
978-1-03-917721-5 (eBook)

1. NATURE, REGIONAL

Distributed to the trade by The Ingram Book Company

TABLE OF CONTENTS

We acknowledge that the Ashnola Valley and Cathedral Lakes Provincial Park is the ancestral, traditional, and unceded territory of Smalqmix and the home of the Lower Similkameen Indian Band.

Pyramid Mountain from Lake of the Woods.

PROLOGUE

I FIRST VISITED CATHEDRAL LAKES Park in 1981 on a hiking trip. My family and I had just moved into the area after many years of globetrotting, and I was keen to see what our new local area had to offer. My son, who was almost three years old at the time, took a whole day to walk the Lakeview Trail up to Lindsey Creek, the boundary of the "core area." We camped for the night before continuing, the next day, to Quiniscoe campground. The hike in, up the Lakeview Trail, left a lasting impression—mostly on my shoulders and lower back!

The purpose of this book is to introduce the general reader to this amazing place. Like most naturalists, though not an expert in any field, I feel I have knowledge I've acquired over the years about the area that would be appreciated by the layperson. All the photographs were taken by me—usually wandering around with a point-and-shoot camera, which is great for hiking, as it is light and fits easily into a pocket. All the species of flora and fauna were taken *in situ*, and I did not search for perfection. I did not import perfect pictures from online sources as most books do. Not all species present are pictured or even mentioned. The photographs are only of what I have seen in my many years of experiencing this marvelous park. It follows, therefore, that any visitor can see the same species and the same scenes, and hopefully experience the same wonder and amazement I have felt. In the past, almost all of my globetrotting was done without much planning, and with hardly any knowledge of what I might encounter. To me, this is the essence of adventure.

In the park, there are many boardwalks and wooden structures to help you cross swamps, bogs, and morasses without damaging the environment or getting covered in muddy water up to your knees. However, the same cannot be said about the morass of self-publishing.

In my joyful ignorance, never having undergone a university education, I blissfully thought that innocently attempting to answer visitors' questions would be relatively harmless. That was before I came upon the misty areas approaching the haunted swamp of *Chicago Manual of Style* formatting. The mysterious woods of the author-date and notes-bibliography system loomed in the background as I bushwhacked through the ankle-deep MLA and CPA.

I had grave doubts that I would ever find the trail. The heavy back-pack of scientific rigour was weighing me down, making me sink below comprehension. So I chose to dispense with it, and instantly became light as a *Parnassian phoebus* floating in a blizzard over a *Sedum lanceolatum*. Now, I use my book as a guide to stand on and keep me from sinking into the morass—and to look up flowers and mushrooms I am not familiar with.

The deep *Chicago Manual of Style* on my boots and gaiters has dried and fallen off. I am ready for adventure again!

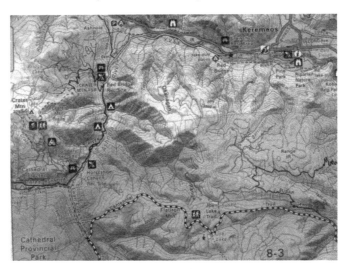

The park is southwest of Keremeos.

Since that first visit over forty years ago, I have camped, hiked, biked, skied, and snowshoed all over the area with family or friends, or alone, all seasons of the year.

I worked as the park facilities operator for the last twelve seasons and gained further understanding, especially of the core area—its visitors, flora and fauna, and spectacular scenery. Many physical challenges exist here, from simply hiking above the tree line to rock traversing and winter overnighting. This area is still very little-known and visited, even by locals, though the experience is world class. This book will not attempt to tell you everything you may come across and so ruin the treat of finding something fascinating for yourselves. It is only a helping hand or a guide to understanding and hopefully identifying various plants and animal specimens, and the nature of the changing landscape. The park is in the Okanagan Mountain Range, just east of the Cascades, about thirty kilometres southwest of Keremeos.

Snow drifting right over the ranger cabin

October on the Rim

This photograph was taken in April after I came up on snowshoes!

Snow drifts in early April

The southern boundary of the park is the Canada -USA border. It's only about forty-eight kilometres directly south of Princeton, but there is no road in that direction. If approaching from the west from Vancouver and the lower mainland on Highway 3, it takes about forty minutes by car from Princeton to reach the Ashnola sign for the Cathedral Park turnoff. You may want to take more time and check out the living museum that is the village of Hedley. If coming from the east, from Penticton or Osoyoos, leave the glorious fruit stands of Keremeos and head west. Just over the first hill going out of town, you will see the turnoff to the left marked Cathedral Provincial Park.

The province of British Columbia has many beautiful parks, but this little gem—in terms of size, compared to Banff or Jasper, for example—compares with the best for its mind-boggling sightseeing locations and sheer variety of ecological zones, with a complete spectrum of flora and fauna, and a great number of rock types.

Down in the Ashnola Valley is a semi-desert with sagebrush and rattle-snakes. If you are going up into the core area, you make your ascent into the uplands of lodgepole pine, ponderosa pine, and aspen. Higher up, you find lodgepole pine and interior Douglas fir. You will then continue higher into a zone of greater moisture, with spruce and sub alpine fir, then through a zone of larch trees and white bark pine, then krumholtz, or "shin tangle," as it is sometimes called, and finally come to sedges, dwarf willow trees, and purely alpine flora. In this part of the core area, at the east end of Quiniscoe Lake, huge amounts of snow are deposited by the winds that blow along the lake. They leave giant drifts on the ranger cabin and road. Around the rim, the constant winds blow the snow away, leaving ice-crusted rocks and a few hardy plants.

I have hiked or driven through all these zones countless times, but I am always impressed by how species have adapted to live in different climates with various amounts of sunshine and moisture. It is almost like having six different countries in one small park.

CHAPTER 1

How to Get There

CATHEDRAL PROVINCIAL PARK IS SITUATED in a geographically interesting location. The westerly winds bring most of the weather systems to British Columbia. Moisture-laden winds from the coast blow inland, bringing rain and snow. However, as the heavy, wet clouds start to rise up from the lower mainland valleys, they cool, and the water vapour they're carrying condenses into droplets of rain. This falls on North Vancouver, of course, and every other town and community, in lesser or greater amounts, depending on elevation and location. As the clouds pass the town of Hope and rise up the mountains through the amusingly misnamed "Sunshine Valley" to Allison Pass (sixty metres higher than the more famous Roger's Pass), the clouds continue to shed huge amounts of moisture. Finally, the storms clear Sunday Summit and drift eastward over Princeton (which, some say, is beyond Hope!). On a summer's day, I have often seen stacks of clouds come over my home in Princeton and disappear before my eyes into white wisps, into blue sky.

Going east from Princeton, it gets continually drier until you reach the only desert in Canada, around Osoyoos, BC. Cathedral Lakes Provincial Park preserves a mountainous area that is on the periphery of the desert to the east side and the interior forest on the other three. The area's geology is unique to it, with huge, granite plutons and the remnants of volcanoes. Dissected by clear streams, sheltering five main lakes and smaller wetlands, the park is truly a gem. It is only about half the size of Manning

Park (about twenty-five kilometres to the west as the crow flies, but about 150 kilometres by road). At 334 square kilometres, it is tiny, though endlessly fascinating.

One of the more interesting road signs.

From the highway three turn-off, you follow the Ashnola Road over the historic Red Bridge. Once a railroad bridge, it was featured on a Canadian postage stamp! Soon, you will see the unique road sign warning you not to run over any snakes that may be resting on the blacktop. Rattlesnakes like to lie on the road to warm up and start their day. They are well-camouflaged and not easy to see, so please drive slowly! From the highway turn-off there is a further ten kilometres of paved road through the Ashnola reserve of the Syilx band of the Okanagan peoples. Pass slowly, going fifty kilometres an hour through the reserve. About a kilometre after passing the powwow grounds, the pavement ends and the gravel road enters a canyon. The yellow kilometre signs are measured from the end of pavement for logging traffic. Use your headlights and drive cautiously, as logging traffic also uses this road, as do other recreational vehicles heading to various campgrounds. The gravel road winds up through two rocky canyons, past two forest service campgrounds, past Ewart Creek Bridge and the road on the left. This bridge is sixteen kilometres from the highway. At twenty-four, you will reach the Cathedral Lodge basecamp.

If you have a reservation for transportation up the hill, or a lodge reservation, this is as far as you go in your own vehicle. If the gate is open, enter and park. If it's not, wait somewhere off the bridge until a lodge driver arrives to let you in. You cross this bridge and park only if you have already pre-booked a ride up the private road. *If you intend to camp in the core area, take cash.* Campsites cannot be reserved, and there are no cash machines up there!

All camping in the park is no-trace. This means not leaving a used or unused fire ring unless it is a park firepit, no garbage, of course, no pile of sticks for the next camper, no piles of spruce boughs to sleep on, no dam in the creek, no picnic plates nailed to trees . . . *absolutely no trace.*

The Lodge Shuttle—one of the ex-Swiss army troop carriers still in use.

3

There are also more comfortable vehicles available! Having got aboard either one of the crew cab vehicles or the ex-Swiss army troop carrier, you'll eagerly await the ride, hoping all your luggage will arrive with you. Unlike at airports, your luggage will at least still be in the same country!

The baggage claim.

The Drive and the Hike

The vehicle first climbs up onto the Ice Age river terraces, then drives along the flat bench, where you may see the crossing of Lakeview Trail, before you arrive at "jump-off corner," where you jump off the flat bench and climb steeply up through a forest of Douglas fir and lodgepole pine. A few twists and turns later, you re-cross the Lakeview Trail twice more before a short descent to Noisy Creek Bridge (the sign calls it this, though it is actually over Lakeview Creek).

The road follows the hiking trail for the next kilometre. As it takes off to the right, the road ascends the steeply sided valley for a while longer until it flattens out at "Sheep Camp." It was thus named because there used to be a bighorn sheep skull nailed to a tree here, which has long since gone. Another flat area follows, with some sand and large granite boulders. Pines start to be replaced with spruce, and the undergrowth becomes thicker as it gets more moisture from both mist and snowfall at this elevation. A short, steep hill brings you up to Lindsey Creek bridge, and your first view of the rim—a grey, rocky ridge still over ten kilometres away.

The road continues tortuously upward to the lodge, after passing through some boggy glades and round some large boulders. With a last, steep hill, you arrive at the lodge parking area, surrounded by mountains and close by the shores of Quiniscoe Lake. The bouncy ride up the hill takes about fifty minutes to an hour. The elevation gain is about 13 hundred metres! If you intend to hike in, then you can pat yourselves on the back for not harming the environment. It is a long and strenuous hike—it will take at least five hours, unless you are exceptionally fit or being chased!

The footbridge over the Ashnola River from the campsite at the start of the Lakeview Trail into Cathedral's core.

Hiking in from Lakeview Trailhead

Passing the bridge to the basecamp of the lodge, continue driving along the Ashnola road, up and over the hill which is usually very "washboardy." Take the next turning to the left opposite the Lakeview Trailhead sign and park at the parking lot (about eight hundred metres). There are three firepits here by the river, and even an old picnic table, if you wish to spend the night or longer before starting up the trail. There are two outhouses on the other side of the parking lot. This is a free campground, and it is not regularly patrolled, so make sure you practise no-trace camping and ensure your vehicle is locked. The notice board has a map and other helpful information. I don't know why this trail is called Lakeview Trail, as there is never a view of any lake, or even Lakeview Mountain, but it is what it is!

As I said, *if you intend to camp in the core area, take cash,* as campsites cannot be reserved, and there are no cash machines up there. Campground fees can be paid in advance on line at discovercamping.bc.gov.ca, but you must bring your receipt or a picture of it on your cell phone. See the chapter on trails and the itineraries chapter for more trail information.

Wall Creek Bridge, the start of "Wall Creek Trail" at kilometre.38.5 on the Ashnola Road

If you don't wish to go up to the core area, you can continue to drive a further few kilometres up Ashnola Road to Buckhorn Campground. This is a large, sprawling campground by the Ashnola River, with a few picnic tables and two outhouses. Camping here is free, as it is only serviced once a week. There are a few nice little fishing/wading/swimming holes here, and it's a great place for kids to explore. Please remember, no off-road vehicles are to be driven around the campground. Fires are permitted in the firepits, but be very careful, as help is miles away if carelessness results in a forest fire. There have been recent forest fires all along this valley.

Ashnola Road continues up to Wall Creek at thirty-eight and a half kilometres on the logging road signs. There are various places to pull off and camp. As always, practise no-trace camping.

A little farther along the road, on the right-hand side, the Centennial Trail comes down the hill from Trapper Lake. The location has changed since the original brochure was printed in 1988. Due to logging practices, forest fires, and general neglect, the Centennial Trail is not that easy to find and follow. Topographic maps and route-finding skills are necessary. The longest journey begins with the first step. So, step onto the Wall Creek Bridge.

Well, now that you know how to get there, and you've decided, perhaps, on whether to hike in, saving both money and the environment, or to take the shuttle and stay at the lodge. You are ready for the big adventure. Have you got everything you might need? Once, a camper forgot matches to light his stove. Another forgot his stove! Seriously—I once arrived at my overnight destination only to discover I had left my tent at home! Make a list before you leave town.

CHAPTER 2

Park Camping and Fire Safety

Be well prepared, even in mid-September!

CATHEDRAL PARK IS A GEOGRAPHIC smorgasbord. There is something for everyone fascinated by nature. The park consists of the lower Ashnola Valley area from Ewart Creek to Wall Creek, and the high-elevation core area. Adjacent to the core area are thousands of acres of tundra-like uplands and mountain peaks in all directions. Here, the experienced adventurer can wander freely and practise no-trace wilderness camping for free. For spectacular locations to practise the art of wilderness camping, try Haystacks Lakes or Twin Buttes. There are sites outside the park, along the Ashnola River, that can be accessed by those who must take a motor home, but even with an RV, *no- trace* still applies.

Only Buckhorn Campground at eighteen kilometres is open to motorized camping. Off-road vehicle operation is not allowed in any of the park campgrounds. Motorized vehicles are only allowed in the Ashnola Valley. No vehicles are allowed in the park—not even mountain bikes, as the impact on the environment would be devastating. Similarly, dogs are not allowed in the park as they would disrupt the wildlife. However, you can park your car and erect your tent down in the valley at Lakeview Trailhead, Ewart Creek, or Wall Creek for free!

If you are hiking into the core area and don't want to hike all day, you will find a couple of nice campsites at Lindsey Creek about halfway up the Lakeview Trail. Along the Wall Creek Trail, you can camp either near the start or about halfway up at the end zigzag, after the last steep hill. Wall Creek meadows are also free, just outside the core.

From the basecamp of Cathedral Lodge at twenty four kilometres from the highway on Ashnola Road, you can either be driven up in relative luxury for a fee, sleep in a comfortable lodge or one of the cabins, and amble around the lake in the sunshine; or, if you choose, you can hike through, as part of a multi-day trail system without shelters or facilities. You can be above the tree line, battling high alpine storms and the possibility of snow in every season. There are places with suggested routes rather than trails, thousand-foot precipices, tundra-like plateaus—places where all one's mental and physical resources must be used to survive.

If you choose to camp—meaning, spending the nights under canvas rather than inside a forty-foot-long motor home—there are only two choices inside the core area. Tenting is only permitted at Quiniscoe Lake and Lake of the Woods. Camping is no longer permitted at Pyramid Lake due to the danger posed by the large number of dead trees. Many have now been removed, though, and Pyramid may re-open on long weekends (to avoid overcrowding). At Lake of the Woods, the danger trees were all felled and burnt by parks staff.

At Quiniscoe, you are welcome to move picnic tables to a more sheltered or shaded position, but please don't leave them in an awkward place or at a weird angle, as there is only one park operator available to move it back, and they are very heavy! Not all tent pads have picnic tables or firepits, so you may have to share. There are only nine

Haystacks Lake is a little more attractive.

picnic tables and thirty sites at Quiniscoe. There are no group camping facilities, as such.

Though there are no real group camping facilities at Quiniscoe, larger groups like the Alpine Club (seen here) seem to manage OK!

Quiniscoe Lake has thirty campsites scattered around the southeast end of the lake. There are four outhouses located around the area. Please leave them as you find them, with the lids down and the door open. This keeps them sweet! Campfires are allowed only in firepits at Quiniscoe. If there is no remaining waste wood from the dead spruce trees, firewood can be purchased from the park operator. Fires are not allowed at Lake of the Woods. Many sites in Quiniscoe have their own firepits, but not all sites have picnic tables, so you may have to share. Some of the lakeshore sites can be very windy.

Lake of the Woods also has thirty campsites. Even if you brought a ton of junk with you on the shuttle, it may be worth walking there, as it is so beautiful.

Just over the boardwalk and you are almost there.

Drinking and washing water are either taken from local springs or from the lake, but should be purified due to the heavy usage by goats, marmots, humans, and so on. You wouldn't believe how many times I have had to tell careless campers this. People have even covered the bed of the creek with leftover rice and beans, and left noodles floating in the lake! I have seen people waist-deep in everyone's drinking water, soaping themselves with shampoo bubbles, saying "It's OK, it's biodegradable!" Well, it's *not* OK! Everything is ultimately biodegradable, but it takes too much valuable space and time.

How to wash dishes . . .
- Take a clean pan, go to the lake or river, and fill it with water.
- Return to your campsite.
- Wash your dirty dishes and utensils.
- Rinse in clean water. Strain out any food particles and put them in your garbage bag.
- Dispose of the wash water by spreading it over the ground, on vegetation. This method protects the water source and the environment.

And now while we are on the subject of hygiene . . .

We know what bears do in the woods, but if you do the same . . .
- first make sure you are a ways off the trail (fifty metres)
- dig a small hole in the duff or ground cover,
- do your business,
- and cover it thoroughly with rocks or leaves.

But . . .
Feel free to pee behind a tree,
Wherever you may roam;
The issue is the tissue—
Always take it home!

*

Lake of the Woods. What a view to wake up to! The Boxcar (to the left)
and Grimface (to the right) from a campsite at Lake of the Woods

Due to its south-facing location, this campground gets more evening sunshine than Quiniscoe. The last rays of the setting sun bathe Lakeview Mountain in a golden glow, while it is almost dark near the lodge. It tends to be quieter at Lake of the Woods, too, as campers who need other people's company—or who have too much to carry or too far to hike—prefer to camp closer to where the shuttle drops them off.

The old cabin at Ewart Creek, a free campsite.

If you're starting your hike in from Ewart Creek, you could also camp there for free. Unfortunately, the historic log cabin at the trailhead has been vandalized, and the area is starting to look like a parking lot for horse trailers. Riders with letters of permission take pack horses on this trail and go on to Haystack Lakes, or the South Slope route to Joe Lake and Snowy Mountain. The old bridge over Ewart Creek finally fell apart a few years ago, but hikers can safely cross the creek about a hundred metres downstream on the metal Ministry of Environment Bridge. Pack horse parties often carry chainsaws, and keep many of the more remote trails—especially in the Snowy Mountain Wilderness Area—open for all. We are very grateful, as without maintenance, these trails could soon disappear forever.

Fire Evacuation

In the core area, below the tree line, there are huge amounts of dead trees, branches, and woody debris from the massive beetle attacks over the last twenty years. This means a much greater than natural fuel load, and as a result, we must all be more aware of the risk of fire—even if it were to be naturally caused, say, by lightning. Therefore, in addition to the stringent rules about campfires, there are pre-planned evacuation routes and assembly areas in case of emergency. There are copies of the plan posted on the registration board kiosk at Quiniscoe Lake and on the front of the ranger's cabin.

Basically, the emergency evacuation plan consists of rapidly following the signs up the Glacier Lake Trail to the top of the hill above the tree line. This is a large, open area where helicopters can land and take people out. This plan is only as a last resort, and for sudden emergencies—if, for example, the road to the lodge is barred by wildfire.

The evacuation zone.

Helicopters can also land on the tiny dock in Quiniscoe Lake, and in the lodge's parking lot.

In 2017, the park underwent an orderly evacuation as the Diamond Creek fire was approaching from the southwest. Campers were asked to pack up and go to the lodge. I and others walked the trails to check for hikers, and everyone was given a ride down the road. There was never any immediate danger to park users, as this prudent evacuation order was given with plenty of time. Luckily, that fire ran out of fuel as it hit the rocky terrain below the Rim trails.

The 2017 Wall Creek Fire (from the USA) came right up to the Rim and ran out of fuel! In 2018, we were evacuated twice. We had pumps in the lake and sprinklers around all the buildings, but again were spared.

15

The Wall Creek Trail was not so lucky!

The view at Quiniscoe Lake the following day.

The Diamond Creek fire in the USA crept over into the Ashnola Valley and down to Wall Creek on the thirtieth of July, 2017. In 2018, there were more fires: Snowy Mountain, Placer Mountain, Cool Creek, and so on. We had to evacuate twice! Again, we dodged the bullet. One day, from the top of Red Mountain, I swept my eyes from the west through 270 degrees. From Placer Mountain to Snowy Mountain was on fire! Only the summit ridge of Crater Mountain was not blue with smoke.

Once, one of the lodge staff left some clothing to dry too close to the woodstove. Even with rapid action on the part of the workers, they lost the cabin. All the fire pumps and hoses were lying ready and prepared for a forest fire, though, so it didn't have the chance to spread. The "rapid attack" crew drove all the way up from the highway, but it was all over by the time they arrived. Global climate change promises more and greater fires, so keep your fingers crossed for the coming years.

There are wildfires almost every year that get close to the park. Even with all the precautions taken by the lodge, it was defenceless before the onslaught of the 2023 fire. On August 16, 2023, two separate fires—the Crater Creek fire and the Gillander Creek fire—were ignored for over a month, as they were both burning with no danger to human habitation. Then, with a few days of thirty-eight-degree weather and some gusty winds, the two fires joined up and exploded into a monster. After a tense wait overnight, the lodge guests and the campers were safely evacuated to basecamp the following morning. A few hours later, the basecamp was gone, and the flames rushed up the valley to attack the lodge. Apparently the lodge and cabins survived, as the fire stopped at the edge of the parking lot. The basecamp and houses down in the Ashnola Valley were not so fortunate, and all were destroyed. The lodge and campground facilities may be gone, but nature will continue to make Cathedral Park an amazing place in the future. It will recover from this, essentially a natural process. Maybe BC Parks will finally be forced to rebuild the outhouses at Lake of the Woods!

Fire pumps in Quiniscoe Lake and firefighters laying hoses and sprinklers around the ranger cabin (2019).

CHAPTER 3

History and Archaeology

THIS AREA WAS COVERED BY ice numerous times through frequent ice ages. When the last glaciations started to melt down in the Okanagan Valley, it left some large blocks of ice that later became "kettle lakes." The remaining ice finally cleared around 10 thousand years ago, leaving scenery bereft of signs of life. Slowly, greenery returned—perhaps a few sedges or bog cotton, then the kind of alpine plants that are now only found on the higher ridges.

Another couple of thousand years elapsed, and the valleys became almost the same as today, with trees shrubs, grasses, and finally deer, rabbits, sheep, goats, and then, eventually, people. They moved up from farther south, following the animals and plants that supported them, and settled in seasonal hunting camps. Traces of these First People's habitations have been found down at Haynes Point on Osoyoos Lake, dating back to around seven thousand years ago. As local human populations expanded and game became scarcer, they made seasonal trips into the Cathedrals area to hunt for food and collect berries and medicinal herbs.

In July of 2019, I was fortunate to find, on the surface next to Quiniscoe Lake, a six-centimetre-long piece of a spearhead, apparently made from local

The Quiniscoe Lake projectile point.

basalt. As there was some patina on the broken piece, it had obviously been there a long time before being broken at the tip. In talks with local First Nations, I have also seen pictures of pecked petroglyphs—more evidence of the continuous use of this area. The main part of the Ashnola Valley is still used for seasonal hunting, as are other areas outside the core. First Nations and others have long-established seasonal hunting camps in the main valley—at the twenty-six-kilometre mark, for example.

There are currently very few berry plants to be found up in the core area of the park. This central area was probably not used much recently for berry-picking, but who's to say what it was like a few hundred or a few thousand years ago? Forest fires pass through from time to time (in 2017, 2018, and 2023, for example), changing the foliage from trees to shrubs, to tundra, back to trees again. Nature is constantly changing! So it is entirely possible that the upper areas could have been huckleberry fields (with a little more rain) or alpine blueberry patches.

In 1860, the International Boundary Survey passed through and noted the high mountains and magnificent scenery. Much later, in 1934, as the story goes, Herb Clark, a young man from Keremeos, managed to save up five hundred dollars to purchase two forty-acre parcels of land from the British Columbia government. He had been hunting and exploring in the Quiniscoe Lakes area for a few years, and decided he would try and start a hunting and fishing lodge and guide service.

*The cabin to the right is Herb Clark's original cabin, built in 1934, with small, flowered penstemons (*Penstemon procerus*) in the foreground*

One parcel was the southeast end of Quiniscoe Lake, and the other was to be "horse pasture" on the ridge between Glacier Lake and Pyramid Lake. I doubt the grass (actually sedges) on that ridge could have fed a packhorse, but that was the idea. Herb eventually built two small cabins by Quiniscoe Lake, and the guests either hiked or rode in with packhorses, up what is now the Lakeview Trail. About halfway up the Lakeview Trail, at the Lindsey Creek campsite, there are still old cabin remains, firepits, and marked trees where horses were tethered.

These cabin remains are about two hundred metres into the core area across the creek

Regrettably, the old packhorse days were a little hard on the environment—also, they needed to practise no-trace camping!

Lindsey Creek. About halfway up the trail is the boundary of the core area. Note the sign on the tree

21

Present-day hikers can still find remains of these old packhorse camps near the start of the Lake of the Woods Trail and around the meadows at the Diamond Trail-Lakeview Trail junction.

Many traces of old horse trails can still be found—the occasional rusty tin can left half-buried, old blazes on trees, and depressions between them where the trail used to be. Not until 1964 did work begin on a road. Around 1969, the acreage above Glacier Lake was sold back to the government in order to bankroll the building of the lodge and work on the road.

Herb Clark formed a partnership with Tom Fleet and Helmut Gehringer (of famous Gehringer vineyards), and Cathedral Lakes Resort, Ltd. was born. The government allowed an easement to connect the company-owned property on the Ashnola River (now the basecamp) to the property at Quiniscoe Lake. Work commenced with the help of Karl Gehringer and an old bulldozer; a narrow, steep road was completed the following year.

In 1968, the provincial government declared the area a "Class 1A Wilderness Area." In 1971, the Centennial Trail, linking Cathedral Park with Manning Park, was marked by these yellow plaques—some of which are still in place!

This one is just below Twin Buttes.

I think it was in about 1982 that the acreage above Glacier Lake was the site of the Darryl Hannah movie *The Clan of the Cave Bear*. A cave was made there and later demolished. All of us old folks remember that! I was working at Nickel Plate Mine at the time, and remember seeing the helicopters taking the film crews up from Apex Ski Hill, where they were staying, to the Cathedrals every day.

In the summer of 1990, Cathedral Lakes Lodge changed ownership to Evergreen Tree Planting Co-op. The lodge is still managed by Richard Patmos, a co-op member.

In spring 1993, the ranger cabin was built on the other side of Quiniscoe Lake from the lodge. This two-storey log structure houses the campground attendant (park facility operator) during the tourist season, as well as visiting park rangers and other workers helping to clear trails and perform other maintenance.

By 1996, the pine beetle had already started to make itself known down in the valleys. Starting around the year 2000, park users noticed that some of the gigantic old spruce, standing as sentinels around the lakes, were starting to lose their needles. A massive infestation of the spruce bark beetle had started. The effects of these infestations are still felt and seen today, with masses of dead spruce trees still standing, and deadfall making off-trail travel all but impossible.

Sauna construction (2018)

Even these ex-Swiss Army troop carriers with chains can't make it up the hill until early June

Between 2008 and 2018, the lodge's guest and staff cabins were renovated. Sawn log siding was put on the plywood cabins. The guest cabins even had toilets installed! The original Herb Clark cabin now has an addition with a bunkbed, and a beautiful, tiled mural around the woodstove, featuring a mountain goat! The outdoor sauna and hot tubs were completed in 2020, but damaged by a chimney fire in 2022. Luckily, the fire was spotted in the early hours and was extinguished before it got too far beyond control. All the lodge's fire pumps and hoses were in place and primed due to the ongoing wildfire danger.

This shows the damaged roof of the hot tub area

As of 2020, the lodge may try and stay open for the winter season. This is not definitive because, Snocats, and the ski-ing public and the climate are all unreliable these days! Will this mean more helicopters, more snow-mobiles, or just more people in general?

Maybe we will have to decide whether parks are for wildlife or people. Will the park in winter be only for the physical and financial elite, who, after having reached the high elevations, can look down on the rest of the world? Should parks be preserved as priceless habitat, or whittled down into subdividable properties for the wealthy? Where will the goats go if they find this habitat unsustainable?

If all potential wilderness users could be persuaded to live and camp more simply, to practise no-trace camping, then greater numbers of people could happily move around the park without causing environmental degradation. Are the few ruining it for the many? The history of the park will continue to be written through climate change, population and demographic fluctuations, forest fires, and other threats to its existence. Sometimes, I feel fortunate to be an old man! We Boomers have had the best of everything, leaving our children and grandchildren with the problems—like this well-equipped young camper!

Rumours

The land across the Ashnola from the basecamp used to belong to a local guy, who owned about 155 acres, almost a quarter section. A few years ago, a Chinese business group bought the land (right next to a provincial park) to make it into a big new resort. Who really knows what they had in mind. Anyway, on seeing what they had purchased, they decided that it would not be possible to build such a resort hotel between the steep bank and the river, so they put it up for sale.

Another group of people decided to form a co-op and buy it, and split it up into twenty lots. Who were they? How did they find out about it? Why was it not part of the protected area? Anyway, it was then covered with a motley mess of houses, second homes, trailers, steel containers, camper units, ATVs, and other unpleasant additions to the wilderness. These buildings were all destroyed in the 2023 wildfire.

The lodge now belongs to Department of the Environment, or BC Parks, so changes may be in the works. Presently, the park gets little attention from the province. The boundaries vary between maps. People illegally cut wood along the Ashnola. Others pull off the road and camp wherever they feel inclined, often leaving a two-metre-wide firepit and sometimes flammables (for the next campers), picnic plates nailed to trees, and other garbage. Over forty years ago, when I first gazed west from the Rim, all was forested wilderness. Now, it's a fire-blackened, clear-cut wasteland with a few green patches. A Princeton company is now chipping up all the wood fibre and making pellets to sell as fuel in Europe. Just how stupid are we to allow this? Will Cathedral Park remain pristine for our children? We must all strive to keep Cathedral Park unspoilt for future generations.

As of August 2023, the latest wildfire will have radically changed most aspects of the park, including the infrastructure and possibly some trail locations. It's the perfect time to improve it for outdoor-lovers of the future.

CHAPTER 4

Geology and Geography

ONE EARLY AFTERNOON IN THE middle of July 2010, I was hiking over the ridge toward Ladyslipper Lake when I heard a loud rumbling. The rumbling became a roar. Looking across the valley toward Goat Lake, I saw a huge cloud of dust rising from the face of the Boxcar. As I watched, house-sized blocks of granite fell from the summit ridge, bouncing and fragmenting in missile showers of hurtling boulders. After five minutes, it was quiet again, and only a huge cloud of dust and a gigantic boulder (see below) at the end of the lake remained to prove I had not imagined it. Although we tend to think of geology as an infinitely slow process, it is going on around us all the time. Gravity never sleeps!

The huge boulder at the end of Goat Lake. The gouge down the slope will be visible for a long time

The summit of Mt. Baker. It's still smoking!

The Local Park Picture

I aspire to open visitors' eyes to the wonders of this area and nature in general. I have always been an amateur "rockhound," constantly picking up rocks wherever I happen to be. I wonder where a particular rock came from, what processes it underwent, and what brought it there. It can be a fascinating story that helps put the present—and even the entire human race—in a different perspective. We are a recent and ultimately very transitory species—a mere blip in the infinity of nature.

I have attempted to simplify the life's work of other, smarter people here in order to provide an idea of the origins of this area. The entire west coast of North America from Northern Alaska to Southern California was all added to the original four-billion-year-old Canadian Shield as part of geologic processes.

Island arcs like the present Aleutian Islands were formed offshore from volcanic vents. As the shield "floated" northwestward on the earth's molten core, these arcs slammed into the West Coast and were forced underneath the shield, rolling up mountains like wrinkles in a carpet. The Cascades volcanoes were one of these wrinkles.

Over hundreds of millions of years, these movements pushed up a series of mountain ranges, many composed of undersea deposits, to unimaginable heights. Erosion by wind, rain, and ice floes wore them down and left thick sedimentary layers of sand and gravel on the plains or ocean sides. Volcanoes covered vast areas with lava—sometimes thousands of metres thick. The process of tectonic plates floating toward the mainland is ongoing, of course. All the little tremors constantly felt in BC confirm this for us.

The "wrinkles" in the carpet are named (from east to west):
- The Foreland Belt (the Rockies)
- The Omineca Belt (the Selkirks and Monashees)
- The Intermontaine Belt (the interior plateaus)
- The Coastal Belt (the Coast Range volcanoes)
- The Insular Belt (the off-shore islands).

The Rocky Mountains were just starting to be pushed upward around 120 million years ago, and the Cathedral area was still warm and semi-tropical. Massive, rain-fed rivers brought down huge amounts of pebbles, sand, and silt from the mountains. Dinosaurs still roamed, leaving evidence of tracks around Tumbler Ridge, and the swampy, tropical forest was preserved as coal beds.

Around 100 million years ago, the granodiorite intrusion that underlies the entire Cathedral Lakes core began, into the "Nicola Group" volcanoes. After all the pushing and shoving of the offshore plates, the southern interior of the province gradually eroded, by weather and frost action, to a fairly low area known as a "peneplain."

About 66 million years ago, a giant meteorite hit the Yucatan. The resultant dust and upheavals killed off the dinosaurs and almost everything else. Luckily, a few rodents living partially underground, like the ancestors of pikas and ground squirrels, who had stored food, managed to survive the devastation. Without their survival and 64 million years of further evolution, perhaps we humans would not be here today!

About 60 million years ago, the pressure from the west eased off, and the Okanagan area was released. It relaxed, creating the Okanagan Valley, which was originally very deep. About 58 million years ago, the Eocene Period began. With the easing of the pressure and the thinning of the earth's crust between 55 and 20 million years ago, molten volcanic rock started to erupt and flow, filling up cracks in the bedrock (see the "dykes" above Hedley, BC), then flowing on the surface. In some local areas, the solidified lava is one thousand metres thick. Again and again, eruptions changed the landscape, often destroying the habitat and covering everything with basalt lava or volcanic ash.

The Eocene was a period when the climate was similar in the area year-round, without the seasonal differences we experience today. The main reason for this was that the Coast Mountains did not yet exist. The peneplain still had to be pushed upward by the pressure of the incoming rocks from the west being forced underneath.

The number of species present in this ancient climate was greater than today, mainly due to the lack of temperature extremes. Where I live, in Princeton, I have experienced plus-forty degrees Celsius in summer and minus-forty in winter—though, fortunately, not every year. Lower elevations in the Okanagan, with the much milder climate, support all kinds of fruit trees and grape vines, most of which can't survive in Princeton. Yet trees like ginkgos and sequoias (giant redwood) grew around Princeton, as did katsuras and birch, alder, chestnut, poplar, and so on. Many of these trees now only grow in the Southern United States and China.

During the Eocene, the topography was still gently rolling, even around the Cathedral Park area. Many places around Princeton and White Lake, for example, had shallow, weed-filled lakes that preserved fossils of the flora of the period in the yearly accumulations of silt from the spring freshet. The flora and fauna in the park location would be the same as the low-elevation forests that covered the lowlands, due to the humid, temperate climate. The Princeton Museum has a collection of local Eocene fossils, some of which are of unique or extinct insect species. The museum is well worth a visit!

As a volunteer with the Princeton Museum Society, I spent many months sorting and identifying fossils from forty cardboard boxes in the basement. All kinds of treasures saw the light of day—including a couple of new species of insects! Princeton has even provided specimens to the Smithsonian Museum.

So, How Long Ago Was That? A Rough Guide!

Epoch	Years Ago	Happening in Cathedral Park . . .
Anthropocene	4,000–Today	Here as elsewhere, many species, including us, are threatened with mass extinction Plastic pollution everywhere Global climate undergoing massive changes Mt. St. Helens erupts (again)
Holocene	3,400	Pristine nature abounds. Mt. St. Helens erupts
	7,300	Mt. Mazama erupts, leaving ash as a white line on a road cut in Ashnola Valley Indigenous camps exist at Haynes Point, in Osoyoos
Pleistocene	10,000	Ice melts in the Okanagan Valley. Still lots up here! Kettle lakes are formed Wildlife and people are moving around
	15,000–1.5 million	First humans reached the Americas Mt. Garibaldi is born (under the glacial ice!) Frequent ice ages, with ice up to two thousand metres deep. Some peaks stick out above the ice (refugia). Some arctic flowers persist!

Miocene	2 million	Ice ages start
	5 million	Coast Mountains start to be pushed upward Coastal volcanic arc starts uplift
	10 million	Original coast range eroded down to low hills
Eocene	36–50 million	Lava flows and ash cover temperate forests. Mt. Baker is born! Removal of pressure allows Okanagan Valley to open up Fossils formed and petrified wood created at Cathedral Park
Cretaceous	55 million	Pacific Rim terrane pushes in from the west
End of Jurassic	66 million	Giant asteroid hits the Yucatan. Fallout causes another mass extinction. Goodbye, dinosaurs; Hello, mammals!
	100 million	Rocky Mountains are pushed higher
	115 million	Dinosaur tracks made around Tumbler Ridge
Jurassic	180 million	Insular terranes are forced toward the mainland, and become islands off the west coast Intermontaine region pushes in from the west Rockies begin to build
End of Permian	245 million	Mass extinction of 96 percent of marine species takes place

Cliff at twenty-six kilometres

Underlying sedimentary rocks overlain with deposits

The cliffs at kilometre twenty-six on the Ashnola Road were made up of conglomerates or possibly boulder clay (glacial till) from very early glaciations. They were deposited on top of older sedimentary rocks. The older rocks were originally laid down as a lakebed—or even an ocean bed. Farther upstream along the Ashnola River, octagonal basalt columns are visible high upon the cliffs above the road. Erosion from weathering and frost action has broken the columns into banks of roadside detritus. As the rocks are constantly eroding, plant life cannot establish a hold.

Basalt columns.

The debris from broken basalt columns can be found along the roadside.

There are many examples of basalt columns in the South Okanagan, some as big as sixty centimetres in diameter and two hundred feet high—Keremeos Columns, for example. The longer it took the basalt to cool and crystallize, the larger the columns. So, if the lava was near the surface, and cooled more quickly, such as at the "Devil Woodpile" in the Cathedral core, then the columns formed are smaller.

Up on the Rim, the Devil's Woodpile is a good example of basalt columns.

This piece looks like a petrified tree trunk.

As the lava cooled, different minerals reformed at certain temperatures. These former layers resembled sedimentary rocks. The lava could have been similar to Pahoehoe lava, which is very runny at first, and forming thin layers of rock when solidified. Many separate eruptions of lava were deposited across the Rim area—hence the layering of the rock, which gives the misleading appearance of sedimentary rock, laid down by deposition from erosion by water .

Another type of lava created these boulders, below the basalt columns of the Devil's Woodpile, and spread across the valley.

*Great globs of sticky, viscous lava rolled down the slopes,
picking up other rocks lying in their path*

Twin Buttes viewed from the meadow across the creek

37

This is a giant-sized bite of columnar basalt that either fell off Twin Buttes or was ripped off by the last glacier and left lower down the valley.

If you hike toward Lakeview Mountain and then take the Centennial Trail over the ridge, you will get to Twin Buttes. These are not exactly buttes, which are found in sedimentary rocks, but volcanic plugs. They are all that was left after these two small volcanoes finished erupting. The lava turned to solid basalt columns. Any soil cover was taken away by the glaciers. The Twin Buttes are well worth a visit. You can carefully climb up each butte, though the rock is quite loose.

Generally speaking, in the Core Area, the rocks are mostly coastal intrusions of three types, grey, slightly gneissic granodiorite,
- mainly reddish, coarse-grained granodiorite,
- light-coloured granodiorite, quartz diorite, and gabbro.

However, the top of Red Mountain is varicoloured andesite and basalt. The top of the Rim is mostly weathered basalt ,except to the south of the fault line, between Devil's Woodpile and Stone City, where it becomes granodiorite (see photo below).

The top of the Ladyslipper Trail is mostly composed of rock formations from the Miocene 2 million years ago, or earlier, the "Princeton group" composed mainly of volcanic ash, shale, sandstone, and conglomerate (also found down in the Ashnola Valley, at twenty-six kilometres).

West of the Rim, below the Glacier Trail area. This area is composed of Nicola Group rocks, containing varicoloured lava, argillite tuffs, lime-stones, chlorite, and sericite schist, dating from the upper Triassic (250 million years ago.)

The contact line between the granite pluton and the volcanic basalt on the Rim Trail near the Ladyslipper junction.

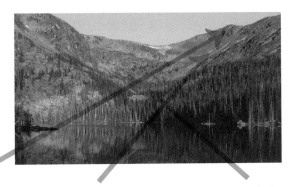

Basalt from later eruptions. White volcanic ash with some fossils. Underlying granite pluton (on top of Waterfall Trail).

The core area of Cathedral Park contains five main lakes, all between 2,000 and 2,200 metres elevation. Three of these lakes—Quiniscoe, Glacier, and Ladyslipper—are headwater lakes lying in a series of adjacent easterly-facing cirques. Pyramid Lake and Lake of the Woods lie down-valley of Glacier Lake. Under the lakes is granodiorite intruded during the Jurassic period (which ended with a bang 66 million years ago!) into the Nicola Group volcanoes. Granite slabs are part of the pluton that is exposed further south of Grimface and the Rim. During the latest round of volcanic activity they got pushed up closer to the surface, where they solidified. Then, over the last thirty million years or so, the ground on top was eroded away, leaving them exposed.

These fossil materials were found in volcanic ash below the Rim.

Looking across the valley above Quiniscoe, one can clearly see the granitic pluton, lower down, up through the top of the waterfall to high up in the hanging valley, where it is covered by pale, white volcanic ash, and above that, various layers of basalt that were once volcanic lava. In the layer of volcanic ash, I have found fossil traces of *Metasequoia*, and even large, deciduous leaves similar to those of birch (*Betula*), over twenty-three hundred metres up! This is way above the present tree line.

I once even found a large, petrified piece of a tree root on the Quiniscoe route to the Rim. Plant life was, of course, all wiped out by the volcanic eruptions and ash falling from the sky around the Eocene period (35–50 million years ago). The area was then covered in vegetation of various kinds, as the climate grew much warmer, without seasonal extremes, and the coast range did not exist.

Petrified wood found below the Rim

I try to imagine what it was like back then, before the volcanic eruptions, a mere 30-50 million years ago, a pleasant woodland alive with many species of trees, from palms to conifers, flowering plants, bees humming, and small mammals and maybe even large mammals like mammoths, mastodons, giant sloths, and then the eruptions started! Imagine the panic, the ground shaking, the confusion, and the inevitable extinctions. Luckily that was a long time before humans got here! When will the next big one happen? We're not here for a long time, just a good time! Did you put a bottle of wine in your pack?

Granitic Plutons and Tor Formations

The layers of Quartz Monzonite granite, being closer to the surface, were subject to erosion from all directions by moisture in the topsoils over millennia. Bear in mind that, 50 million years ago, the Coast Mountains did not yet exist and the climate was less variable and much wetter. Microscopic cracks and weaknesses were widened by actions of moisture, dissolving the granite surfaces. At Stone City, there were widened cracks in the granite that filled up with water borne minerals that left seams of quartz up to 5 centimetres wide running through the rocks. Erosion began when the granite was underground with water seepage and continued above ground with windblown sand, frost, and rain all impacting on it.

This is on the Ladyslipper Trail down from the Rim

These granodiorite intrusions were originally molten granite up to 30 kms. under the surface

Looking across the "grus," one can see the line of paler volcanic ash at the top of the Ladyslipper to Rim Trail

Because the tors were eroded from all sides, they are rounded. All the material that eroded off is called "grus," a quartz monzonite sand with no fine silt or clay particles and a pH of 5.6. It is extremely porous and a very tough habitat for flowers or even moss to grow in.

The Giant Cleft

The Giant Cleft was originally a small crack in the granite pluton forced apart by volcanic rock pushing in from below, like toothpaste. That filled the crack with molten lava, which widened it and split it even more. The intruding rock was softer than the enclosing granite. So, over millions of years, it was worn away. Eventually, over millions of years, of snow and frost and rain and goats the softer volcanic rock eroded away leaving this *huge* crack, with a spectacular view over the trail down to Ladyslipper Lake.

Near Grimface, you can still see the lava on top of the granite

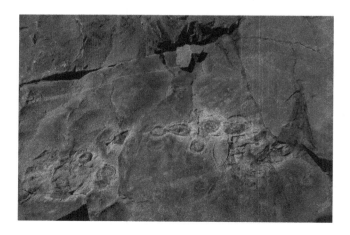

Intrusions? Or fossils?

These may possibly be marine fossils from the Triassic Period that were pushed up by the incoming Quesnelian arc from the west. These are in the rocks below the Rim on the Glacier/Rim trail. Ancient sedimentary rocks were metamorphosed by the Eocene volcanic upheavals. Above this layer is metamorphic rock, and again above that are the volcanic rocks that may have originated after the Eocene (see below).

The Ypresian Period in geology is part of the Eocene. The lake bed deposits around Princeton and all the way to Republic, Washington were laid down in the Ypresian Eocene Periodic (40-54 million years ago). They contain many fossils of plants now found only in temperate areas of the world. The Coast Range did not yet exist we can conclude, as this area had many more species in the Eocene Period and the climate was much warmer, wetter, and less seasonally variable. The greater seasonal variation in temperature, the fewer species of flora and fauna—even insects!

Ancient sedimentary rocks were metamorphosed by the Eocene volcanic upheavals

Glaciation and Its Consequences

During the Pleistocene Epoch, this entire half of the continent was covered in an ice sheet up to a height of twenty-three hundred metres. The flow of the glacial ice was toward the south and southeast. As the Similkameen

Valley lay across this angle, it was probably filled with static ice; hence, its present-day appearance, with generally low banks on the river. From Keremeos, however, the valley was widened, straightened, and deepened by the ice movement as the valley turned and pointed south.

There were many ice ages, some more widespread and longer-lasting than others. At times, ice covered the entire area as far south as the Columbia River, to a depth of thousands of feet. We usually only see the landforms left after the most recent glacier melted, sometime between twelve and ten thousand years ago. Some ice ages merely filled the valleys and left some of the higher peaks as "refugia," where unique specimens of flora and sedges managed to survive. Because they were isolated for thousands of years from their "kin," they became distinct species—for example, Cusick's speedwell. It is slightly different from other speedwells and only grows in this park.

As the major ice ages ended, the giant glaciers slowly left behind the boulders they were pushing or carrying and melted away, leaving glacial erratics like the ones pictured below. In places, huge, stranded blocks of ice melted to form kettle lakes, like Swan Lake in Princeton.

Granite erratic on Glacier to Rim Trail, resting on Quesnalian metamorphosed sediments (i.e., from the Quenalian arc that was born 400 million years ago far off the west coast, then pushed east and began "docking" with the west coast around 170 million years ago!).

This is definitely a glacial erratic piece of granite, right on the basalt summit of the closest Twin Butte. Red Mountain is in the distance

Soon, the only glaciation left was up where the snow fell beyond the winter season. This snow compacted into the last glaciers, which filled the cirques below Macabre Ridge and Grimface, below Smokey the Bear, and below the Rim above Ladyslipper and Glacier Lakes. The weight of thousands of feet of ice moving relentlessly downward deepened the valleys, which then filled in with the melting ice, and lakes were formed. As the glaciers moved down the valleys with their load of eroded rocks, they sometimes dammed the original lake outlet (like at Ladyslipper Lake) and made a new one! The end of Quiniscoe Lake was dammed also with a terminal moraine, as were Lake of the Woods and Pyramid Lake. Sometimes, there was a naturally-occurring hill of bedrock that diverted the melting glacier, leaving wetlands—on the Lake of the Woods trail, for example.

Landforms

The lakes; Quiniscoe, Scout Lake, Pyramid, Glacier, Ladyslipper, and Lake of the Woods, were all at one time carved out and formed from glaciers that moved over the mountains. As the glaciers pushed slowly downhill, their weight gouged out the lakes and left smoothed areas of rock behind (like the smooth slabs below the Rim on the Ladyslipper Trail, and underneath the base of Smokey the Bear). As the glaciers slowly melted, the vast amounts of rocks they had pushed aside were left behind as lateral (at the sides) and terminal (at the end) moraines. The mounds of broken rocks at

Scout Lake and Glacier Ridge, and even the campsite at Lake of the Woods, are examples of moraines.

Existing outcrops of rock caught up the rocky debris as it slowly pushed by and built up the ridges. When the ice finally melted, valleys flooded with meltwater, carrying huge amounts of rocks, gravel, sand, and mud. As you drive down the Similkameen Valley, you can see "kames," or river terraces—almost-flat bench lands above the river. These were once the valley bottom, until rushing meltwater re-scoured the valley, making it deeper. The number of terraces may correspond to the number of ice ages, but who knows how many went before and left no trace, as their terraces were erased by later ice ages?

Smokey the Bear

The Giant Cleft from Ladyslipper Trail.
It looks small from here!

Sometimes, the glacial meltwater floods blocked the valleys with debris, and as the meltwater flood lessened, a lake would be formed behind the dam. As the run-off entered the lake, the current would slow, losing the energy to carry larger pebbles—only fine silt.

A small example of this can be seen from the jeep road as you ascend the first steep hill from the parking lot at basecamp. The old lake or pond bed received another covering of fine floodwater silt every year, leaving these lines as proof, over ten thousand years later! When the lakebed was further cut into after the ice age dam was breached by a flood, these layers would become visible. These are usually seen as almost horizontal lines in the sand, called "varves."

Varves

Eventually, the dam broke and the lake drained out down the Ashnola Valley. This part of the road is now a few hundred feet above the bottom of the Ashnola Valley. These banks are very fine mud and silt. The water was, therefore, almost static, as it did not have enough energy to carry even small rocks. The erosion continues. How much lower will the river go before the next glaciations or volcanic eruption, or the next mountain building uplift? Observe the large rocks in the Ashnola River and consider the energy needed to transport them!

Solifluction

This is what happens when saturated soils and rocks flow downward. There are many examples of this phenomenon throughout the park. Some date from the melting of the last ice age, and some more recent slides are still moving! Gravity never sleeps! This photograph was taken on the Diamond Trail, close to the junction with the Lakeview Trail. Check out the inclination of some of the trees as they move down the slope.

Solifluction. Moving rocks and trees

More Solifluction.

Patterned Ground

Patterned ground

This is a network formed by a mixture of frost action and erosion. Vegetation finds it very difficult to establish itself, as the surface is constantly shifting. This example is above Scout Lake on the Centennial Trail. In the distance is the summit ridge of Crater Mountain, which has a pond with amazing patterns—almost-circular patterns of rocks and small gravel that freeze and thaw under a shallow pond

Crater Mountain Pond

Other Geological Oddities

Which combination of natural forces creates these large, round holes in granite glacial erratics? Are they formed by small rock particles going around and around, eroding the solid rock over thousands of years? Any ideas? These weird holes in the granite can be found along the summit ridge of Lakeview Mountain. It is well worth the effort it takes to get there. The views are outstanding—almost otherworldly.

For those who like to name natural phenomena, how about the "devil's washbasin"?

Large, round holes in granite glacial erratics

As a teenager, I spent all my spare time hiking and rockclimbing on Kinder Scout, the highest point of the Peak District in Derbyshire, in the UK. These weird rocks on Lakeview Mountain were also present on Kinder's north edge, where I have a rock climb named for me! Millstone grit, the rock local to the Peak District, is very similar to Cathedral granite, which would also have made excellent millstones to grind grain into flour. The rocks on Kinder are also eroded by the wind into fantastic, rounded blocks and towers—very spooky on a misty day! That must be why Lakeview Mountain is my favourite Cathedral hike. On Kinder Scout, I remember it was always raining or misty, and brutally cold. How fortunate we are in Cathedral Park, where the climate is almost always perfect for hiking!

CHAPTER 5

Trails and Itineraries

TERRAIN AT ALL ELEVATIONS IN the park is almost infinitely variable, as is the weather, so here are a few words about being able to cope. If you stay down in the valley close to your vehicle, you can ignore this advice. However, if you are going into the core area, take note: the wilderness doesn't care about you; you have to look after yourself!

1. Is your clothing suitable? Dress in layers, wickable underwear—not cotton, except in summer at low elevations. Cotton gets wet with perspiration, becomes heavy, and takes forever to dry. As cotton clothing dries, it makes you colder. Have at least one insulating layer (fleece or wool, not cotton).
2. Have a wind shell or raincoat.
3. Have a wool or fleece toque and mitts (even in summer, if going up out of the valley).
4. Have a stick or walking/hiking pole. (Or two!)
5. Wear water-resistant boots with stiff soles. On the Rim trails, you may have to cross snowfields, and you will need all of these items! If you have to cross a snowbank, you'll want to be able to dig the sides of your boot or your heel into the snow. This can't be done while wearing running-shoe-type footwear. Long-distance runners, take note!
6. Don't leave the lodge area for a walk unless you have a small daypack containing such items as: water bottle, emergency clothing

(mitts and toque), wind shell, and a whistle. This is the minimum, so that if you sprain your ankle, you can at least stay warm until someone better prepared can help.

A longer list could include a power bar or two, a bright-orange garbage bag or space blanket, a headlight, matches, fire starter, Swiss Army knife/Leatherman tool, a first aid kit, and a topographical map. Most important of all, common sense!

A few years ago, two people were lost for three days. Helicopters flew over hourly, and over a hundred search-and-rescue volunteers combed the park for them. They were not injured, and they only needed to stand in the open to be seen, but didn't.

Directions in this book are told from the point of view of you, the hiker—for example, "to your left is a large granite boulder," or, "the trail goes to the right." It may be useful to say to one person, "to the southwest," or to give a GPS location, but some people don't even know which way is up! If you're really in doubt about which way to go, retrace your steps. Then you will be sure to get back to where you started.

The core area.

Almost all the trails are gently angled, and they often zigzag. The trail up to the Rim from Ladyslipper Lake has been used and abused by man- and goat-kind for generations; therefore, there are many steep stretches. But careful observation usually reveals a zigzag to make your ascent or descent easier. When going up or down a steep hill, smart people zigzag. Changes of direction make the climb less steep—you have better traction and an easier time of it. Zigzags also minimize erosion of the trails, keeping them easier and safer. Don't be misled by the mountain goats—fitter, with better balance, sharp hooves, and four-wheel drive, can often go straight up or down! So don't be a goat! Stay on the zigzags and don't cut corners.

When on the trail, add a rock to any cairn you pass. This makes the trail obvious. If you are not sure if you are on the trail, then don't make cairns, as they can be disastrous after a few inches of snow—people may leave the trail and lose their way! A large, visible cairn is a lifesaver in a heavy snowstorm.

The Ashnola River runs in a very deep, scenic canyon. Entering this canyon from Keremeos is a little like entering the Khyber Pass. (Yes, I have been there!) I imagine, before the road was built, it must have been almost impossible to get up the valley during the highwater of spring run-off. No doubt, when passable, the First Nations, and later, gold-seeking miners, used the valley bottom trails to access the high country and alpine meadows.

There are five ways to access the high country. . . .

A. Using the Lodge's Shuttle for a Fee (see Chapter 1)
B. Following the Lakeview Trail to the core area.
C. Hiking the Webster Creek Trail to Snowy Mountain Wilderness Area, via the South Slope.
D. Taking the Ewart Creek Trail to the core area via Twin Buttes or via Haystacks Lakes.
E. Exploring the Wall Creek Trail to the Core Area and Centennial Trail, or the "climbers' route," to the south of Grimface.

B. The Lakeview Trailhead

This trail begins down a turn-off about two kilometres past the lodge base-camp on the Ashnola River Road. At the end of the turn-off, there are two or three tenting sites with firepits, two outhouses, and a parking lot. You can camp here for free!

Get an early start in the morning. Cross the Ashnola River by the footbridge and start up the trail. After a couple of zigzags, you ascend to a benchland (see Chapter 4), and then up again to emerge onto the private road. The trail continues along the road for a short distance before taking off again to your left and continuing up through the sparse pine and fir. The trail ascends, steeply, crossing and re-crossing the road. Eventually, you cross the road next to a couple of huge, granite boulders. These came off the cliffs to the left and rolled down many years ago. A few yards further is a more recent wanderer that rolled down in 2010—you can still see the pathway it ploughed through the small trees!

The rock still blocks the trail, so please move it if you can!

A short while later, you hit the road again, turn right, and stroll, thankfully, downhill, to "Noisy Creek" (actually Lakeview Creek), a good place to fill up your water bottles for the trail ahead.

The trail now follows the private jeep road up a very steep hill, around a corner past a grassy flat, then relentlessly upward again. At the top of the next hill, the trail takes off to the right, leaving the road for the last time.

Noisy Creek bridge.

Now hiking up an old logging road, you hopefully find pleasure in being close to nature again. From the parking lot, the first two or three kilometres are probably the steepest—so don't be disheartened. Eventually, you will reach the sign for Lakeview Trail.

Leave the old road and ascend the trail

If you were to continue on this old road, you'd come out at "sheep camp" on the jeep road. As you go up to Sage Ridge, you get your first views of the Cathedral Range after climbing up a pleasant part of the trail. In 2020, careless campers left a campfire near here that took four water bombers and a ground crew of twenty to bring under control!

Sage Ridge

Another few kilometres and you push through the heavily pine-beetled forest into an area that is usually swampy up to the banks of Lindsey Creek.

As this used to be a hunting and horse packers' camp, there are many remnants from large camp-fire rings, and even the remains of cabins. A large muskeg meadow opens up here, and the moisture level increases again. There is usually snow here until mid-May or later.

Lindsey Creek

Crossing Lindsey Creek into the core area, the trail winds up through the forest. A few kilometres more and the tree types change to mostly pine and spruce, before you emerge into the alpine meadows just below Scout Mountain. At the junction, Diamond Trail goes off to the right. This trail is easily followed in summer, but almost impossible to find in winter, as the deep snow hides all the trail markers. A short downhill over some boardwalk and flower-filled glades brings you to the turn-off for Scout Lake. This is a scenic, shallow pond about two hundred metres to the right.

At the bridge over Scout Creek

You have arrived at the lodge!

Continuing onward from the junction, mostly downhill through pine and spruce forest and meadows, you hike another couple of kilometres and reach the clear-cut area around the lodge. The large spruce trees around the lodge were all cut down after they died from the spruce bark beetle infestation and became a safety and fire hazard. Head down the hill to the left, cross the jeep road, and make your way to Quiniscoe Lake campground, or continue to the left another fifteen minutes on the trail to Lake of the Woods. Now, relax—you deserve it!

C. Webster Creek

To get to Webster Creek, take Ewart Creek Road. From the highway, drive about sixteen kilometres. Ewart Creek Road is a minor road to the left that crosses the Ashnola River, then turns right and continues about two kilometres to the junction of Ewart Creek and the Ashnola. About two hundred metres past the last cottage on the left, there is a sharp, left-hand corner and a small parking spot on the right. If it is occupied, or you need more room, go a little further along to park your vehicle, and walk back.

*Leaving the benches at the
bottom of the trail*

Now, on the uphill side of the road, there is a sign asking ATVs to stay off the trail. This the start of the Webster Creek trail. The trail starts right from the sharp corner.

A few steps farther is a large, granite boulder with a brass memorial plate bolted to it in memory of a local outfitter. Follow this steep trail up onto a grassy bench in the sunshine. This benchland is an old river terrace or kame left here when the last glacial ice melted and brought all the mud, clay, and boulders down the valleys about ten thousand years ago. The trail crosses this bench and ascends to the left, onto another bench. It goes along this bench to the south, then climbs again, steeply, on long zigzags, to a rocky corner overlooking the Ashnola River and Webster Creek. Finally, there is a slight downhill as you turn toward Webster Creek, before steeply ascending into the trees. This is a steep trail, and mostly very narrow—especially lower down the mountain. It picks its way up the rocky slopes and goes up the side valley above Webster Creek.

In mid-summer, this can be an extremely thirsty experience! I once hiked up here, with a full backpack with everything our family needed, at noon, when it was thirty-eight degrees Celsius in Keremeos. Nowadays, when hiking a long distance, I try to start early in the morning—though this is not always possible. Once you are out of the valley and into the trees, it's not so bad. Carry enough water!

After an hour or so of following the trail up through the trees and crossing a fence line, you thankfully break out onto "Starvation Flats." Some friends christened this upland meadow's name, as their little boy was starving for his lunch! It is a beautiful grassland area with great valley views. Depending on the season and the presence of grazing cattle, the trail can be a little indistinct, as it makes its way to your left and then slightly uphill across the meadows, toward the trees. This area has many giant, old Douglas fir that are either dead or dying. As a result of the winter winds, many trees are down and the trail is hard to follow. Look for old, grass-covered ruts and sawn logs!

Gaining elevation constantly, the trail emerges after a zigzag from another patch of Douglas fir and pine grass, eventually, into a wide meadow area. It drops down to meet the main trail coming from the left (uphill). Far below is the Ewart Creek drainage. A short distance farther brings you to a fence line, gate, and tiny creek—the only water to be found on this trail.

The creek at Sheep Station, a group of vintage log cabins built in the fifties and owned by the University of British Columbia, where scientists occasionally take up residence to study the sheep

A Sheep Station cabin

If you're camping here overnight, be sure to take a slow hike up Flatiron Mountain, which rises behind the cabins. A great evening stroll gives views across the valley to the peaks of Haystacks Mountain, the end of the Boxcar, and the summit of Lakeview Mountain. You may even see some sheep! This vast grassland is known as the South Slope. This is an awe-inspiring natural grassland, and a very popular horse packing campground. It makes a great place to camp for the night. A few years ago, a fire was set above here to create more grazing for the sheep—however, it took off, and half the mountain got burnt off. It is still recovering; so be very careful with your campfire!

Backtracking to just before the gate and creek, a trail goes off to the left, up the meadow. After about two hundred metres, you see an old A-frame cabin that can also be used to overnight—very useful in winter! The trail continues upward to Joe Lake. This is the start of the World Ridge hike that goes around to Harry Lake,

The A-frame cabin

Newby Lake, and the summit of Snowy Mountain—a world-class trip!

It takes about a week, and is all glorious alpine scenery— mostly above the tree line!

Descend below the cabins on the trail toward Juniper Creek. The trail drops steeply to the far right into the trees again, across Juniper Creek, to join the Ewart Creek trail.

The South Slope, with happy hikers

D. Ewart Creek

If you drive to the very end of the Ewart Creek Road, you pass a couple of private outfitters' cabins. After about two kilometres, you see an outhouse, a horse corral, and a dilapidated old cabin.

The bridge that used to cross the creek was in such a state of disrepair that it was dismantled in 2015. However, about fifty metres downstream is an aluminum bridge that can be crossed with care by walkers only. Once across the creek, follow the well-defined trail that follows the it upstream for about four kilometres. It passes interesting forest glades, then some very large, granitic rocks, until eventually arriving at a wide, wooden bridge over the rushing torrent.

This crossing is made over an old bridge

This was built in 1991 by the students of Rutland Secondary School. Jim and Alex Terbasket and Clarence Schneider brought all the equipment and supplies up here by packhorse. Be careful, as the bridge has seen better days! This takes about an hour and a quarter from the Ewart Creek cabin.

Up the rocky trail, after another ten minutes, you proceed to the junction, with the Sheep Station trail that turns off to the left and crosses Juniper Creek. You can now cross Juniper Creek on a cable car.

Stay to the right and continue upward. Pass the base of a rockslide, through some nice camping meadows and up sandy switchbacks. Eventually, after about four kilometres, the trail leaves Ewart Creek and ascends Mountain Goat Creek to the right, toward Twin Buttes. About five kilometres up this creek, there is another trail going off to the left that goes to Haystack Lakes. On the main trail, the Centennial Trail, the Cathedral core area can be reached.

As you enter the wide upper valley, with Twin Buttes to your right, you may see the occasional yellow Centennial Trail markers. The trail follows the edge of the old growth, between the dwarf-willow-choked swampy ground and the forest. Many small, new trees have grown in. Do not be tempted to cross the willow swamp, to the visible clear, grassy areas on the other side. The horse packers and hunters have made various camps on those meadows, and they now have a private cabin over there.

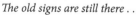

The old signs are still there . .   *. . . even if they're on the ground*

Horse packers and hunters' private cabin,
across the creek from Twin Buttes

The meadows above the outfitters' cabin

(a) Centennial Trail

The Centennial Trail was made in about 1971, and has not been well maintained. It is on the top edge of the clearing on the Twin Buttes side of the wide upper valley. The trail comes up the valley in the trees, well below the bare rock debris. After you have passed the closest butte, follow the trail up to a large meadow. This is a good place to camp. You will, however, have to make your way down to the creek for water.

Hike to the most westerly end of the grassy area. I flagged this trail in 2020 up from the Ewart Creek drainage sign to the line of cairns above the tarn.

From the open meadows camping area, hike south across the upper creek swampy area, through small larch up onto the bare hillside. Go straight up the low grass and sedges, until you can see a line of rock cairns heading uphill to your right. You may see a small tarn from snowmelt (usually dry after August), above

which the cairns are easier to follow. Follow the cairns up to the shoulder of the ridge whence you can see the lodge and the core area. Down the other side of the ridge, the trail is hard to see, so follow the cairns until you meet the Lakeview Mountain Trail coming down from your left and see the sign reading, "No horses beyond this point." Then, simply follow the trail all the way down to the creek, up the other side, to join the main Goat Lake Trail back toward the lodge.

The good camping meadow is to the left of the closest butte. Once back on the main Lakeview Mountain trail, the lodge is visible right across the valley, still about two hours away. Please follow the trail! With all the deadfall, trying to go straight toward the lodge would be impossible.

Looking back down the line of cairns from the top of the ridge.

The ideal campsite at Haystacks Lake— no-trace camping, of course!

(b) Haystacks Trail from Ewart Creek

If you continue from the Ewart Creek Trail on the trail that takes off to the right, then another four kilometres gets you to the beautiful Haystacks Lakes. Only one is deep enough for fish, while the other two almost vanish in really hot summers.

From Haystacks Lakes, it is still a long walk to the core area. There isn't a trail—just a route! Around and above Haystacks, you really feel in the wilderness. You are on your own!

Hike out from the most southern and westerly of the lakes (the deep one) and ascend to the ridge up the grassy areas. Keeping the prominent Haystack "nipple" to your left, proceed along just below the ridge.

Summit Ridge. Incidentally, it's quite an easy scramble to the top of this volcanic plug if you don't mind loose rock

Monoliths

From Haystacks, hike along the ridge until a gap opens up, and you can descend between giant monoliths, amid stunning scenery.

Down through the gap, you will hopefully see the line of cairns and goat tracks that lead down toward the head of the valley. There are two small rocky peaks, visible on topographic maps, over and around which the route passes before descending over sparsely treed, rocky ground to the head of the creek, below the back of the Boxcar. Once you are on the barely visible trail, you should see the park sign on a stunted tree.

I was too lazy to carry the standard, eight-feet-long, treated, wooden four-by-four post over here! I only hiked over with the sign and a drill. I still wonder how I managed to carry a full, treated post, sign, and tools all the way up to Stone City (incidentally, passing a few groups of hikers on the way)!

Continuing to the head of the creek, there are a couple of gorgeous camping spots, more or less outside the core area. The route to the core area goes to the left on the horizon, then veers right up to the top of the Boxcar. When looking toward the back of the Boxcar, the route goes up to the lowest point, then follows this low point

uphill to the other side of the Boxcar, from whence you can see the goat trail down to Goat Lake.

Here is the location of the good campsite. The creek has water in it if you follow the course downstream a couple of hundred metres

Lowest point of the trail, campsite on the right

This is an overview from partway down the back of the Boxcar. The trail comes from the giant monoliths on the ridge, and goes around these little humps. Haystacks Mountain is the little bump at the left end of the ridge. There is a large vale between the front part of the ridge and the peak.

The trail from Haystacks comes over the lowest part of the Boxcar It then follows a goat track just below this ridge. At the col, turn left to get down to the Goat Lake Trail, or keep going along the ridge to join the trail over Lakeview Mountain.

From above the campsite

The Boxcar from The Lakeview Mountain trail

E. Wall Creek Trail

This trail will take you to the core area, the Centennial Trail, and the "climbers' route" to the south of Grimface. Continue driving along the Ashnola River Road, past the Lakeview trailhead, past Buckhorn campground, all the way to kilometre thirty-eight. Shortly after kilometre thirty-eight, to your left, you will see a small parking area and a huge wooden footbridge. Wall Creek Trail is part of the Centennial Trail, which goes from Manning Park to south of Cawston. The Wall Creek Trail is solely a hiking trail, and thus is very narrow as it slowly winds its way up the Wall Creek drainage, through open lodgepole pine and aspen forest.

You may encounter lots of deadfall across the trail, depending on recent weather and whether the Parks Department has cleared it. This trail is part of the Centennial Trail that is included in the annual "Fat Dog Run," a one-hundred-mile event from the Ashnola to Allison Pass. The deadfall of winter is usually cleared by the volunteers helping the run organizers. The lower parts of the trail have a couple of landslips—the sandy soil slipping down toward the creek—so be careful.

In the hot, dry summer of 2017, a wildfire started in Diamond Creek, a tributary of the Ashnola River in Washington State. A few weeks later, it had made its way as far as the base of Wall Creek, but left some patches unburnt.

At higher elevations, the fire crept up the grass in the gullies and almost made it up to the Rim Trail. Thankfully, though, it never quite got over the crest and into the core area.

In 2018, there were even more disastrous fires, and many surrounding creek drainages were charred. But things will grow back.

The junction with Centennial Trail to the left (the "Fat Dog" route) and to the right the old "climbers' trail" that goes to the south of Grimface

A few years ago, a friend and I voluntarily spent two days clearing the deadfall off this trail to the right. We cut five hundred trees on the way up, and we only got as far as the swampy meadows below the back of Grimface. It was not much fun, carrying tents and camping equipment, plus chainsaws, tools, gas, and oil! I would like to see volunteer groups undertake these trail clearances on

Some sections of the Wall Creek Trail really changed with the latest forest fire!

a frequent basis. Maybe someday, I will do some more myself, if I have the time.

The Centennial Trail to the left goes to the lodge at Quiniscoe Lake, the heart of Cathedral Park. After the junction and a couple of steep zigzags, the trees start to thin out, and you enter the lower part of Wall Creek meadows. As the meadows open up, you cross another little creek and start to see cedar boardwalks, which protect the muskeg—and make walking a lot easier! Though covered with dwarf willow shrubs, these swamps would be tough going without these.

The boardwalks take you through the muskeg and up into drier areas, with shorter grass and sparse trees, to the edges of Red Mountain meadows. You go up and over a dry hillside, past a "Core Area" sign, then down slightly to a usually tiny, almost-dry creek. Looking up to your right, you can see a gap in the mountain range. This gap is directly above Quiniscoe Lake. If you take a steep diversion above here off-trail, and a short, steep climb bearing to the south (your right) will take you up onto the Rim Trail, from whence you can carefully descend to the left of the snowfield, if there is one, onto the route down to Quiniscoe.

This cuts about four kilometres off the regular Centennial trail, which goes all around Red Mountain. There is no trail over the ridge, so only experienced route finders should try this!

If you're staying on the main (Centennial) trail, cross the tiny creek and wend steeply upward and to the left as the trail skirts Red Mountain. After some steep parts of the trail, you emerge onto a flatter, boulder-strewn area with views to the east. Crossing the boulder field carefully as it veers to the right, you join the Diamond Trail, which comes in from your left. There is a signpost here. Stay to the right here, and climb up the grassy and rocky hillside until the vast view to the south and east opens up before you. About a hundred metres to your left is a picturesque little tarn at the base of Scout Mountain.

Grimface, and the Rim in the distance, the view from the tarn

A little farther along the trail, you come to the junction and signpost of the Rim Trail to the right. Looking carefully over the cliffs on your left, you can see Scout Lake a few hundred feet below.

Scout Lake is very shallow, and you can sometimes see the tracks of moose that have waded right across it. Descending now along a zigzag trail through the larch trees,

Scout Lake from above

you soon get back down into lodgepole pine and meet the main Lakeview Trail. Turn to the right and continue along toward the lodge. Only about another two kilometres to Quiniscoe and a well-deserved rest!

Exploring the Core area

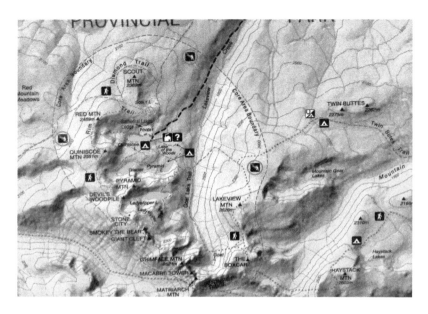

The core area.

The vast majority of people these days seem to come up on the "shuttle," spend a couple of nights either in the lodge or camping, and then get a ride down. The first full day is usually a hike up the Glacier Trail from Quiniscoe Lake to the Rim. They then hike left along to Smokey the Bear, back along to Ladyslipper Lake Trail, and back down. The second day is often the long hike up to Lakeview Mountain. On the third day, the Diamond Trail is considered an easier option, and any extra time is usually taken up with fishing, resting, checking the local wines, or attending to blisters. If this is your plan, then the following is what to expect

The Rim from Glacier Lake Trail

Starting from Quiniscoe campground, follow the trail just above the camp-ground toward the waterfall at the end of the lake. After about fifty metres, a trail sign appears on the left for the glacier trail,(and the fire evacuation route sign), and you start up the hill, soon passing a giant block of granite on your left. The mountain goats often use this trail, so you may see droppings on the ground or wool on the lower branches—especially in July. After a few zigzags, you encounter a small meadow area. There are usually many spring flowers here, such as Cusick's speedwell, a tiny, blue flower with oval leaves. Leaving the larch trees (feel how soft the needles are compared to spruce!), you come out onto open moorland with extensive views over Glacier Lake.

The trail is rocky, but please keep to it, as the vegetation gets damaged otherwise. Dropping down slightly toward the lake, you pass the junction with the other Glacier Lake Trail that starts near Pyramid Lake and is the easiest way to the Rim from Lake of the Woods campground. Crossing a tiny creek (usually the last good place to fill your water bottle), you climb again through the few remaining larch trees onto the talus slope below the Rim. Carefully following the trail, adding a rock to the cairns, you finally reach the right hand end of a rocky band. Follow this rocky band up step-like ledges to the left.

Depending on the season, you may encounter snow here. This is why boots are recommended rather than soft running shoes. With boots, you can dig the heels and sides of your feet into the snow. If there is a lot of snow, it is sometimes too dangerous without proper equipment. If the rocky steps are still snow- and ice-covered, then go to the far right on the broken rocks to go up around it. Be warned: do *not* venture up these steep rocks if they're covered in ice or snow. The ice can be hard, with water running on the surface, and crampons can be necessary!

Once you are above the snow, follow the trail and cairns over the whitish ash layer up onto the Rim, to the trail sign. Vegetation is sparse here, and there are many visitors, so please try to stay on the trail. Goats are often to be seen in this area. Please, do not approach them to take pictures, as constant disturbance from people will habituate them, making them a nuisance rather than an amazing sight to see!

The route goes over metamorphosed rocks of the Quesnalian arc, then conglomerates, into volcanic ash (see Chapter 4), and finally, onto a trail again. Through dwarf alpine vegetation, you reach the main Rim Trail at the signpost. On a clear day, you can see Mt. Baker in the distance! Now, wasn't that view worth the effort?

Mt. Baker

From this point, you have a decision to make. Either turn left to follow the rim along to the "Devil's Woodpile," then toward Ladyslipper Lake; or turn right, going over the summits of Quiniscoe Mountain, then Red Mountain, back to the lodge area via the Centennial Trail.

Kelowna Secondary School brings students up every year to experience the wilderness on their doorstep. Here, they have reached the summit of Quiniscoe Mountain on the Rim Trail. I think the slower one, to the right, was probably a teacher!

The Lakeview Mountain Trail and Goat Lake

The Lakeview Mountain loop is a fairly strenuous day—depending, of course, on your level of fitness and the weather conditions. Allow between seven and ten hours to do the hike.

From Quiniscoe or Lake of the Woods, take the trails that go toward Goat Lake. At Pyramid Lake, take the trail toward Ladyslipper. After about a hundred yards, you reach a junction and signpost. Goat Lake Trail goes to the left, Ladyslipper Lake Trail to the right. Follow the left trail through fairly open spruce and pine forest (most of the spruce are dead!). Eventually, the path descends fairly steeply, through four zigzags, to another junction. Here, you can see an old blaze, and directions carved into the tree right at the junction. Nowadays, we try not to damage the environment.

"Goat Lake" and the arrow, were carved into the tree by horse packers

Stay to the right, drop down into the valley, and follow the creek all the way up to Goat Lake. Eventually, the valley opens out. You get spectacular views of the peaks around Grimface Mountain. Goat Lake is an easy hike, mostly following a rushing stream, and there is some amazing scenery—and of course, lots of flowers.

Those brave souls who tackle the Grimface Traverse climbing route head up to the lowest point on the ridge, and then go right. Do not even attempt without proper climbing gear and experience. It is not a rock scramble.

Just before you reach Goat Lake is the turn-off, to the left, to Lakeview Mountain. From the signpost on the Goat Lake Trail

Goat Lake and Denture Ridge.
The Boxcar is to the left

(which points to the left and uphill), turn sharply left and cross the creek by the large boulder. The barely visible trail crosses the swampy meadows toward another house-sized boulder. Then, at another large boulder, the trail becomes more obvious, meandering in very wet zigzags up the steep hill through giant old spruce trees (mostly dead!) and finally into a more open and drier larch forest.

Looking back down the trail toward Goat Lake

Ascending through the larch, you emerge onto a huge bowl of dry granite boulders and sand. You will often see tiny alpine wildflowers here that will amaze you. Follow the indistinct trail upward to the col between the Boxcar (to your right) and Lakeview Mountain (to the left). The tiny red dots on the online maps that designate a "route," rather than a defined trail, are pretty inaccurate.

The view from Lakeview Mountain trail at the Boxcar col

At this col, you can turn left for the Lakeview loop or right for the Boxcar.

Goat trails from the col to the Boxcar

If you're going right, to the Boxcar, the highest goat trail draws closest to the cliffs at the top and usually has less or no snow. There is even an emergency bivvy shelter under the rocks! This is the route between Haystacks Lake and Lakeview Mountain.

If you're going up Lakeview Mountain, follow the goat trails and small cairns to the left over and around the rocks, uphill for about a hundred yards, until you come over the top onto a small, flat area. Here, the trail crosses the ridge and the sidehill, slowly gaining elevation over rocky terrain until it turns left again and ascends over rocks to the summit ridge. There are a few small cairns that mark the way. Look for them, and add to them, as this route is not that obvious! Once this ridge is gained, fantastic views open up all around. By carefully looking for small cairns and tracks, you can make out a trail heading across and up the final few hundred yards to the summit, the highest point in Cathedral Park.

Lakeview Mountain summit

On the summit, follow the trail to the right (east), toward the other "summit," then head left again, proceeding to descend between the two high points through rocky meadows. There follows an impressive, long descent across broad hillsides, with panoramic views, until you arrive at a junction and a sign ("no horses beyond this point"), almost at the tree line. The Centennial Trail goes off to the right, over the ridge behind you, toward Twin Buttes.

A little lower, you see and hear the creek rushing down on your right. This is a great place for a rest, and to fill up your water bottle.

Isn't this a little piece of paradise, with all the spring flowers?

There are usually lots of ground squirrels running around here. The trail now descends, at first through grassy meadows, then through pine groves, and finally back into the dead spruce and balsam fir mix. Due to the dead spruce, there is a lot more light coming in, so the growth of fireweed and other foliage is rampant. The trail crosses numerous wooden walkways and tiny creeks until you arrive at the bridge over Lakeview Creek.

Now begins the long uphill climb back to the Goat Lake trail junction, then up again to the right toward Pyramid Lake. It's only about twenty minutes of steep uphill, but it can seem like a lot more! Once up the hill, you are soon back at the lodge or your campground.

The Diamond Trail

The Diamond Trail

The Diamond Trail is a loop that goes from the main Lakeview Trail into the park, which joins the Centennial Trail, coming around to rejoin the main Lakeview Trail, just a few hundred metres from Scout Lake. I always prefer to do the Diamond Trail in an anti-clockwise direction to avoid labouring up the zigzags.

Starting from the lodge, go up the road and take the turn-off to the right. Continue on this trail, past the first turn-off (Centennial Trail), then past the Scout Lake turn-off. Crossing the wooden bridge, continue up through the heavily pine-beetled forest until it starts to thin out into patches of ground-squirrel-filled grasslands. Then, you cross over a couple of wooden walkways to emerge from the trees into beautiful alpine meadows, with views to your left of the end of Scout Mountain.

Upon reaching the Diamond Trail sign, turn left and follow the narrow trail through alpine meadows full of flowers, and across a couple more walkways over small creeks. This area was a favourite of the old packhorse

85

campers, who left a few sawn branches and buried firepits. However, all the giant spruce died, and the area is being re-greened with fireweed, arnica, and other flower species, in addition to subalpine fir. The trail meanders down into grassy dells below the end of Scout Mountain, then starts to climb a little through the trees until you emerge once again above the tree line, with far-ranging views north.

Diamond Trail fireweed   *Diamond Trail flowers*

The last couple of years saw scary views of the approaching wildfires in Cool Creek!

A little farther, the trail leaves the trees entirely and crosses a loose, rocky area before climbing again, next to some larch trees, then joining the Centennial Trail. At this junction, make sure you stay to the left, as the hike down Centennial Trail to Wall Creek will leave you thirty-eight kilometres up from the paved road and about twenty-four from basecamp! From the junction, you huff and puff steeply over the hillside until you are granted the amazing view across the tundra of Grimface and the other peaks around Stone City. A tiny tarn can be seen to the left of the trail. Lake of the Woods is shining in the distance, and Grimface is to the right.

Follow the zigzags down to rejoin the trail you came up on

A big storm coming up the Ashnola!

Continuing on the trail, you arrive at the top of the cliff overlooking Scout Lake, and the junction sign for the Rim Trail up to Red Mountain.

Red Mountain and the Rim

This is a shorter version, letting you experience a little of the Rim without doing the whole thing. To do it in a clockwise direction, start by walking to the end of Quiniscoe Lake. Cross the sagging boardwalk after the rockslide, then cross the little bridge over the creek. Just around the corner is a turnoff to the left, up to the waterfall. From the waterfall base, you go to the right, up the hill, via a series of easy zigzags. At the top, you can go to the left and clamber over bare granite rocks for a scenic lake view from the top of the waterfall. Or, you can stay to the right and continue upward on the narrow trail entering the hanging valley—usually a riot of flowers.

The view from the upper hanging valley, looking back toward Lakeview Mountain, with a glimpse of the Boxcar. Potentilla is blooming in the foreground

Follow the trail up past the larch trees and cross a tiny creek to the base of a rocky pinnacle. Do not follow the goat track up the gulley to the left. This is quite steep, and goes up a slippery slope to the head of the gulley, then goes left over broken rocks into another hanging valley. Instead, you can stay right and zigzag up the hill, then head left to rejoin the trail. This is a great place to stop and be amazed at the great walls of rock around you—look across and see the layers of ash and volcanic rocks!

Carefully cross through the long grass, look out for the ankle-breaking holes between the rocks. Blame the hoary marmots! Continuing upward, you approach an outcrop of rock. You can go along a rock ledge and up, or skirt around to the left and up.

On top of the rock, continue upward, and hopefully you will see a few small cairns leading to the right, with a small trail. The goats, of course, go straight up or down, and the snowfall changes this slope every year. I have been trying to maintain a trail that goes up to the right, but it depends on the snow. Most years, there is a big, vertical snow cornice here, and it can only be crossed on the far-right side until late July or so! So, please be careful, whether you're going up or going down.

The snow cornice above Quiniscoe (stay to the far right!)

Finally, you emerge onto the Rim. The sign is your reward! From here, you can go to the right, up Red Mountain, or turn left to ascend Quiniscoe Mountain and the continuation of the Rim Trail.

Or, if you are going down to Wall Creek, you can bushwhack down the hill, bearing slightly to the right. You may have to wander around a little to avoid loose, rocky areas before finding the little Wall Creek Trail crossing the open grassland.

If you turned right toward Red Mountain, go up the rocky slope carefully until you are on the summit. Follow the indistinct trail until you have passed all the summits. The trail then drops down to the right of an outcrop. You may be able to see the trail crossing the tundra far below. Look out for rock cairns as you descend steeply, over large rocks, to this area of tundra. The trail then crosses this bench, dropping lower to the left, until it reaches a junction with the Centennial Trail. Turn right to return to the lodge, or left to go around Diamond Trail loop or down the Centennial trail to Wall Creek.

Snow Season in the Core Area

Snow season can start as early as mid-September, but realistically, the winter season is from November to April or late May. Starting in 2020, the lodge might be open in winter, according to an article in *Powder Magazine.*

On the west side of the Rim, on the Centennial Trail coming up from Wall Creek

The main issues for the park are access and snow coverage. I have skied in up the Lakeview Trail a number of times—which, as you may imagine, is a tough slog. There is often a lot of deadfall to be negotiated, and the trail markings are sparse in some areas. Only as you emerge from the forest near the junction of the Diamond Trail does it become worth the extreme effort. Don't forget—you'll be carrying full winter camping equipment!

My only skis are old Fischer 99s, which have steel edges, but are very narrow. With skins, though, I can climb all day. It's going down that can be the problem! Contrary to the impressions given in *Powder Magazine*, I have to say, Cathedral Lakes Park is not a great place for backcountry skiing. After horrendous climbs up to the Rim, it is usually almost bereft of snow, as it blows constantly, leaving only a very thin sheet of ice, with occasional deeper drifts. It's always very icy—and so windy that ice particles from your skis blow into your face!

Once, in spring, I hiked in, expecting all the snow to have melted. It was clear of snow until I reached Lindsey Creek and found the snow. I kept going, following large, deep moose tracks. Around 2 p.m., I realized that I was very tired, stepping into snow almost a half a metre deep every other step. I was trying to stay under trees, where there were patches without snow. Around 3 p.m., I realized that if I didn't act soon, I would not be able to return to my car before nightfall (around 7:30). Using my Swiss Army knife, I cut two small spruce trees and bent them double to form a rough snowshoe. With some nylon cord from my pack and duct tape from around my water bottle, I attached three cross branches to each loop, and after some trimming and adjustment, I had a pair of snowshoes! These enabled me to hike through the open meadows to the Diamond Trail junction, then down toward Scout Lake junction. There, at a lower and more sheltered location, I was able to make good progress again, and reached the lodge area around 4:30. As the lodge employees come up frequently in winter, the road was hard packed by their snowmobiles, so I managed to jog down the road to the Lakeview campground in a couple of hours! So, I hiked the round trip to the lodge and back in about ten hours, through snow that was almost a metre deep in places. The moral of the story? Be prepared, don't overextend yourself, and give yourself plenty of time. All the usual stuff!

Heading into the ranger cabin, with the drifting snow up to the roof!

Some of the trails are visible from Quiniscoe Lake, such as the Lake of the Woods loop. Depending on the amount of deadfall, you may make it. Skiing across the lake is easier than trying to find the trail. Goat Lake trail is hard to follow in deep snow, but as soon as the valley bottom is reached, one can ski almost anywhere, as all the low shrubbery is covered. This is below the cliffs of Denture Ridge and some of the gullies the adrenalin junkies of *Powder Magazine* have skied down.

The Goat Lake Trail used to have this large snag overhanging it

Near Goat Lake, back country skier sheltering among the giant boulders along the Lakeview Trail in order to cook some lunch

This outhouse sign is about 1.75 metres high   *The apparently dead trees are actually small larch, which lose all their needles in winter*

All good things must come to an end. When going down the Lakeview Trail to your vehicle in the Ashnola, you'll find the first part, to the Diamond Trail junction, pleasant enough.

Centennial trail near the end of Red Mountain

Incidentally, going along the Diamond Trail gives access to some nice, easy lines down into the trees; however, they are not very long. Going down the trail to Lindsey Creek is still not too bad; there is a fair amount of space between the trees, and it's not too steep. About a kilometre below Lindsey Creek, a short climb leads to the top of the real downhill. The narrow trail, often invisible between the trees, drops steeply, with many turning challenges. It is very easy to lose the trail here in deep snow!

The Sage Ridge area is comparatively easy before you drop down to the old logging road. The rest of the trail down is easy to follow, but can be very challenging due to deadfall and rockslides. Eventually, though, you get down to the parking lot for the Lakeview Trail by the Ashnola River. Having done it a few times, I am strangely not anxious to repeat it!

The road is private, so if you wanted to ski down or up the road, you would need permission. The lodge is in business to make money, so be prepared for a refusal.

In summary, there are many, many places to experience backcountry skiing in BC. There are many areas with much easier access and better slopes and snow. Some places even include helicopters, food, and lodging. If I had that kind of money to spend, I would go somewhere else!

In summary, Cathedral Lakes Provincial Park, because of its location between Manning Park, Snowy Mountain Wilderness, and the wilderness areas of the United States, provides unlimited opportunities for all kinds of adventures and exploration.

Washington State is full of hiking trails that used to come all the way up into Canada and join the Pacific Crest Trail. Alas, that seems to be just a dream these days, and I fear that many trails are being left deserted, becoming overgrown or covered in deadfall or wildfire debris.

So get out there and make a difference, clear an old trail, explore a new area. Get out there and really live!

CHAPTER 6

Flora

FLORA CAN BE DIVIDED INTO trees and shrubs, flowering plants, grasses and sedges, ferns, mosses, liverworts, and lichens. However, vast as this subject is, I must limit my interest to what one is likely to notice in Cathedral Park. Due to the vast range of "biogeoclimatic zones" there, many different species have made the park their home. The differing elevations—from two hundred metres above sea level in the Ashnola Valley to over twenty-five hundred metres on top of Lakeview Mountain—provide habitat for many different species of flora.

There are many excellent flower books on the market, so I am only including some of the more frequently occurring species in Cathedral Park. Most of the species shown here are found around the lodge and higher up the mountains. Flora found down in the valley are common throughout this area of BC, while the alpine flora are quite unique. Few people get up to the core area before the middle of June, due to the snow on the road preventing the lodge's vehicles from using it. Those that hike in can get to see the early spring flowers that others may miss, but not to worry. Spring doesn't start in earnest up there until July, and there are still some blooms into late September.

Biogeoclimatic Zones

A "biogeoclimatic zone" is a geographic area with similar patterns of energy flow, vegetation, and soils as a result of a broadly homogenous macroclimate. There are various systems in use to delineate these zones. The BC Ministry of Forests, the World Wildlife Fund, Environment Canada, and the BC Ecoregion classification all have their own preferences. All of these are confusing systems that sound extremely complicated to me. In this book, my purpose is to help answer questions rather than create new ones!

Starting from the highest elevations, I am calling these zones . . .

1. Alpine Tundra
2. Subalpine to the Timberline
3. Lodgepole Pine and Subalpine Fir
4. Engelmann Spruce and Subalpine Fir
5. Interior Douglas Fir
6. Bunchgrass Meadows and Ponderosa Parklands
7. Modern Plantations (which are predominantly lodgepole pine)

These zones are mostly named after their predominant species, but contain the habitats of many others. Some species are very widespread, and can grow almost anywhere, whereas others are more choosey.

Each of these zones has its own flora. Usually, these species are found only in that particular zone, because the precise needs of the species, in terms of nutrients, water, sunshine amounts, even fungal mycorrhiza are only present in that specific location.

Alpine Tundra

This zone is characterized by extremes of climate, quality of soils, and temperature differences. A plant may grow behind a rock because it could not survive without the heat reflected off the rock. There are some areas (for example, on the Boxcar Mountain Trail) where almost nothing can grow on the shattered granite sand. To help them survive, many plants have incredibly deep and wide-reaching root systems. Look here for tiny alpine lupines, moss campion, and umbellate pussypaws. Places with some kind of soil, such as below the summit rocks of Lakeview Mountain, have grassy meadows that look like grass but are actually sedges, like the Carex and Kobresia species. On some of the damper tundra locations, there are also very tiny trees. Alpine willows only one centimetre high can be found near some of the summits.

Subalpine to the Timberline

This zone is probably the most productive in terms of eye-catching flowers. Grassy, flower-filled meadows and glades occur between the larch trees and the white bark pines of the subalpine. The location is a little more sheltered, so the flower stems can be taller without blowing over! Look for the heathers, phlox, moss campion, and showy Jacob's ladder.

Lodgepole Pine and Subalpine Fir

Still high elevation, but fairly dry due to the exposure to wind, sunshine, and porous soils. This is not so much a "zone," but pockets that exist in certain areas, such as around Lake of the Woods campground and Pyramid and Quiniscoe Lakes. In shadier and north-facing sites, this merges into Engelmann spruce and subalpine fir.

Engelmann Spruce and Subalpine Fir

The most obvious flowering plant here is the white-flowered Sitka valerian (*Valeriana sitchensis*) for most of the season. Early on, they are pinkish. After the valerian fades out, they are followed by yellow arrowleaf groundsel (*Senecio triangularis*). Growing in damp areas and springs are saxifrages and many other species. Look for rare white shooting stars (*Dodecathion dentata*) along the path around Quiniscoe Lake. The other zones are located lower down the mountain and into the Ashnola Valley. Notable are the bunchgrass meadows above Webster Creek Trail and across the Ashnola Valley, on the south side of Crater Mountain.

Interior Douglas Fir

This zone is from the Ashnola River, on the shady side of the mountain, all the way up to Sheep Camp, on the road to the lodge. Many of the fir are diseased and falling over. It seems it is getting too dry for this species. Around China Ridge Trails near Princeton, the droughts of the last few years are having the same effects. The lessening rainfall over the last fifty years is turning this zone into grassland!

Bunchgrass Meadows and Ponderosa Parklands

These areas are the winter homes of mountain sheep. This zone is mostly just above the Ashnola River. On the sunny side of the valley, these parklands run right up Crater Mountain.

Modern Plantations

The ministry calls them "forests," but these are as different from forests as a wheat field is from a meadow. Very little understorey is present, and very few flowers, except on the perimeters—and these are often invasive species, such as knapweed and hound's tongue.

In addition to elevation, many other factors, such as the amount of water or sunshine, the steepness of the land's slope, its underlying rock type and exposure to wind, and the amount of traffic (human or animal) can all influence the kind of flora to be found. Even tree girth can vary enormously depending upon where the tree is growing.

Outside the ranger cabin is the stump of a subalpine fir that was about 160 years old when it was cut. It was a dead danger tree and had to come down. It was in a good growing location with plenty of water and sunshine, and a sheltered position. Compare the size (about forty centimetres in diameter) with a small slice of larch tree inside the cabin—which, though seventy-five years old, was only about seven centimetres in diameter.

I often wonder about the ages of other plant species that I encounter. How many years does it take for a plant like moss campion to establish itself and grow under such extreme conditions of soil and climate?

In the following pages are a number of the more common species to be seen, along with their location and date of blooming. The various flowers, shrubs, and trees are arranged in order of colour only. Any further classification is beyond the scope of this book. Some plant genera contain many species. For example, there are at least four different species of arnica, and a few of sedum, daisies, fleabanes, and so on. Trying to identify the specific species can be very difficult, even with a botanical textbook. Sometimes, experts in the field disagree over what is a species and what is not. Recently, with new DNA technologies, many plants (and fungi) have been placed in quite different families than they once were. There are many excellent books on the market that can help with further identification (see Appendix). I have often spent hours trying to pin a plant down to a single species.

Colours can be paler or more pronounced depending on the age of the flower and how much rain or direct sunlight it has had to put up with. Trees are identified after the flower section.

White Flowers

Long-stalked Starwort
(*Stellaria longipes*)

Usually found under Douglas firs. Look for the unusual blue-green colour of the leaves. This plant grows in patches under Douglas fir on the Diamond Trail. It is only about ten to twenty centimetres tall, and blooms in early August.

Cascade Skycress
(*Smelowskia ovalis*)

Shelters under rocks in the high alpine, especially on the Boxcar and Lakeview Mountain Trail above Goat Lake. These flowers are found at very high elevations, trying to stay out of the wind! They bloom in early August. Just look at the soil in this picture—it's a wonder it can grow at all!

Bog Cotton
(*Eriophorum angustifolium*)

Grows in swampy areas—for example, near the boardwalk to Lake of the Woods. It blooms around mid-July. Both these plants are about thirty centimetres high.

Bog Orchid
(*Platanthera dilatata*)

Grows in the same wetland as bog cotton, and blooms about the same time. With grass-like leaves, these fragrant flowers can be seen in the wetlands around the boardwalk to Lake of the Woods. They bloom around mid-July.

Sitka Valerian (*Valeriana sitchensis*)

Grows under spruce trees between Quiniscoe and the Glacier turn-off. These plants are up to a metre high and prefer shady, cool, damp sites. They develop a very recognizable smell. Early in the season, the flowers have a pinkish hue. From July onwards, they are along all the lower trails.

Alpine Bistort
(Bistorta vivipara)

Can be found in the high tundra on the Rim. It is only about ten centimetres tall, and easy to miss! It can only be seen when it is in bloom in August, as it is so small it blends in with the sedges.

Globeflower (*Troillus laxus*)

This beauty is a kind of white buttercup usually found in damp areas in June and July (what passes for spring at 2,000 metres elevation!). Note the buttercup-like leaves. Often, it grows profusely around springs and wet, swampy areas, like below, at the outflow of Glacier Lake.

Western Pasqueflower (*Anemone occidentalis*) or Alpine Anemone (*Anemone drummondii*)

Also called "mop tops" after flowering, as the seeds have long, grey hairs, giving the plant a "mop top" look. "Hippie on a stick" is another Kooteney nickname! Prairie crocus is a similar species, but is usually pale blue/purple.

Marsh Marigold *(Caltha leptosepala)*

This plant likes water so much it even submerges itself in it; I caught my own reflection here, too. Flowers are about three centimetres across, and the leaves are almost round. That's how you can tell it's not a globeflower.

Fringed Grass of Parnassus (*Parnassia fimbriata*)

Easy to spot when not in flower, as it has egg-shaped leaves that almost look like little green bowls around the stem. These impressive blooms are usually found in damper areas under the trees around Quiniscoe, where they bloom in mid-August.

Fescue Sandwort or Thread-leaved Sandwort (part of the genus *Eremogone*)

Similar to its *Minuarta* relative, this sandwort has basal—grass- or hair-like leaves. There are quite a few plants similar and related to this species. They are found in drier, rocky places between the alpine zone and the forests, and bloom in June and July.

Spotted Saxifrage (*Saxifraga bronchialis*)

Saxifrages are a very large family! There are nearly 400 different species worldwide, with more than thirty in the alpine zone. For the spotted kind, look on the petals for tiny pink spots!

Brook Saxifrage (*Micranthes odontoloma*)

This saxifrage grows by streams or seeps. The leaves are almost round, and the white flower heads are tiny.

Western Saxifrage (*Micranthes occidentalis*)

This kind has larger, leathery, rounded leaves.

Tufted Saxifrage (*Saxifrage cespitosa*)

This kind has spots on the petals, and the leaves have three lobes.

Drummond's catchfly (*Silene drummondii*)

Here are two types of catchfly (*Silene* species). This is also known by the common name "bladder campion." The balloon-shaped structure below the flower gives it away. It is not always easy to identify the exact species. The flowers open at night, and close during strong sunlight. Some are pollinated by moths!

Pearly Everlasting (*Anaphalis margaretacea*)

Usually found in the forest undergrowth, in the lower subalpine. Obviously, these flowers are a favourite with these metalmark butterflies. The flower heads can last all winter.

Cow Parsnip
(*Heracleum planatum*)

Prefers damp areas where there is some surface moisture. It's about a metre or more tall. The stalks are hollow.

Indian Hellebore
(*Veratrum viride*)

Another plant found in damp areas, all parts of this very noticeable plant are poisonous! Before I knew that, whenever I needed to fill my water bottle, if there was only a tiny creek, I used the leaves as a funnel! These spectacular plants can grow over a metre high, and the stalks last into the following year.

White Shooting Star (*Dodecathion dentata*)

This one isn't even in my flower books! They grow up to twenty-five centimetres tall, but don't bloom until mid-July. The only place I have ever seen them is by Quiniscoe Lake Trail, on the shady south side.

Five-stamen Mitrewort
(*Mitella pentandra*)

This strange-looking plant has green threads instead of petals, and is found on damp, shady slopes. It is more of a transparent green colour—take a close look at those stamens, they're really cool!

False Solomon's Seal
(*Smilacina racemosa*)

Up to a metre tall, this plant likes low to subalpine damp areas. It has red berries later, like clasping twisted stalk.

Canada Violet
(Viola canadensis)

Also found at mid to low elevations. The first part of the Goat Lake trail has them. Look for the purple-ish lines on the lower petals.

White-flowered Willowherb *(Epilobium lactiflorum)*

This plant is of the same genus but a different colour than both Fireweed and Hornemann's willowherb,

White-flowered Shrubs and Berries

Common Snowberry *(Symphoricarpos albus)*

About a metre tall, this deciduous shrub has smooth or wavy-edged oval leaves. It is also known as waxberry, and is fairly common lower down the mountains and in the Ashnola Valley. The berries aren't edible.

Mountain Avens (*Dryas octopetalis*)

Forms most of the ground cover on high, rocky ridges. The leaves are very easily identifiable. They are about a centimetre and a half long and ribbed. Avens bloom in June on Ladyslipper Trail to the Rim. They also form wispy tops when gone to seed.

Partridge-foot or Mountain Spirea (*Luetkia pectinata*)

A similar ground cover, whose tiny leaves resemble partridges' feet.

Common Elderberry (*Sambucus canadensis*)

Grows below the tree line in damp areas, producing lots of dark blue berries. There is another species that has red berries. Both kinds are found near the lodge. They may have been introduced by horses—one of the reasons that horsemen are no longer allowed in the core area, as they can bring in all kinds of seeds in horse droppings. This is also what happens with off-road vehicles, which can introduce unwanted, invasive species, such as knapweed, into the alpine.

One-sided Wintergreen (*Pyrola secunda*)

These flowers only grow on one side of the stalk! They are found in damp places, like the trail up from the creek to Lakeview Mountain. As you walk through the woods, you may find this plant near tiny springs.

The following are actually shrubs or trees, but initially, the most noticeable thing about them is their white flowers, which is why they are here rather than in trees and shrubs!

Trapper's tea (*Rhododendron columbianum* or *Ledum glandulosum*)

Found all around Lake of the Woods. Not to be confused with "Labrador tea," which looks very similar, but is brown and woolly under the leaves. If you make tea with the dried leaves, don't drink more than a cup, as the alkaloids can cause cramps and even paralysis!

White-flowered Rhododendron (*Rhododendron albiflorum*)

A tall, many-branched shrub with very pliable branches and glossy leaves. Known as "mountain misery," it is extremely difficult to try go uphill through it! It grows in between spruce, and only below the tree line. It can be found on the righthand side of the trail from Quiniscoe to Pyramid, below the big rock slide.

White Heather
(*Cassiope mertensiana*)

Found trailside between Ladyslipper Lake and the Rim. It grows to about twenty centimetres high

Saskatoon
(*Amelanchier alnifolia*)

Also known as serviceberry, this small tree is usually only about two or three metres high, so the fruit is easy to pick—and no thorns, either! It only grows at low to mid elevations. The white flowers emerge in late April down in the Ashnola Valley, and lots of purple fruit later on.

Dwarf Alpine Willow *(Salix* species)

These are trees! Many different species of willow grow in the alpine. Some have bright orange catkins, some have red, some brown, some green. In the alpine, they are only centimetres high, but they reach up to a metre or two down in the valley below Goat Lake.

Slide Alder
(*Alnus viridis*)

Along with various scrub birches (like *Betula glandulosa*), these grow down in the wetter and more sheltered Goat Creek Valley—and of course, down in the Ashnola.

Grey Leaf Willow (no photo)
(*Salix glauca*)

Yet another type of willow, these grow very low to the ground. They can be found in Goat Creek Valley with the scrub alder.

Yellow Flowers (from palest yellow)

Round-leaved Alum Root (*Heucher cylindrica*)

The alum component in the leaves was used by First Nations to stop wounds from bleeding. This plant grows at all elevations, but prefers drier ground.

Yellow or field locoweed (*Oxytropis campestris var. cusickii*)

Found at lower elevations, usually in grassland areas.

Arnica

This genus has seven species in this geographic area. They have ray flowers around a yellow or brownish centre, like small sunflowers. A careful examination of the leaf shapes and flower heads is necessary to identify their species. Let's just call them all arnicas and enjoy them! Those pictured are probably broadleaf arnicas

Northern Goldenrod
(*Solidago multiradiata*)

Found mostly above the tree line, often on rocky ground. Yet it grows all over BC in many environments.

Lance-leaved Stonecrop
(*Sedum lanceolatum*)

Just one of the two species that grow up in Cathedral Park. The fleshy leaves can be eaten (in moderation), especially after a fall frost.

Few-seeded Draba
(*Draba oligosperma*)

There are many draba species, including the few-seeded draba. This is like the stonecrop, insofar as this plant seems to manage without any soil! These have four petals and hairy leaves, and are found on the barren tundra. Apparently, the only way to tell the species with certainty is to study the different-shaped hairs on the leaves with a hand lens. *Draba incertaour* has similar petals, but different, hairy leaves.

Round-leaved Violet
(*Viola orbiculata*)

Found in the damp woods going down toward Goat Lake. Look for brown stripes on the petals.

Golden Daisy
(*Erigeron aureus*)

Has spoon-shaped basal leaves and blooms in mid-August. These flowers are much smaller than the arnicas.

Egg Yolk Packera
(*Packera pauciflora*)

Lacks ray flowers—just has an orangey "yolk." These are in the Aster family, and probably survived through the ice ages in a "refugia" above the ice.

Lyall's Serpentweed
(*Tonestus lyall*)

Pictured here growing with penstemon and a species of fleabane. The rocky ground is amazing in its floral abundance! This is just below a rocky outcrop on the Diamond Trail.

Towering Lousewort
(*Pedicularis bracteosa*)

Pictured a little late in the season here (late July), so the bloom is almost over! These are very interesting plants, as they are partially parasitic, taking nourishment from the roots of surrounding plants. They prefer slightly open grassy areas near pines, and can be found near the junction of Diamond Trail and the Lakeview Trail to the Ashnola.

Arrow-leaved Groundsel
(*Senecio triangularis*)

This plant takes over after the sitka valerian has faded, before the lupines. Found along the trail to Pyramid.

Western Paintbrush
(*Castilleja occidentalis*)

This species of Indian paintbrush has yellow bracts and grows lower down on the Lakeview Trail, in the sagebrush area.

Once again, the following species are mainly shrubs, but as the flowers are so obvious, I have kept them in the flower section.

Cinquefoil (*Potentilla* species)

A very large genus with hundreds of species worldwide, about a hundred of which can be found in North America. There are quite a few in this area! You can tell them apart mostly by the shape of their leaves, which vary from palmate with three lobes to numerous leaflets along a midvein. Some have exactly five leaves, as the name suggests. They are found all over, in clear areas at or below the tree line. Lots of potentilla grows on both sides of the Quiniscoe to Rim route, above the waterfall. Recent advances in DNA research have changed a lot of the Latin names. So, some plants that used to be known as potentilla species are now known by other names. Most are usually seen in a shrub form.

Yellow Mountain Heather (*Phylodoce granduliflora*)

Grows on the Ladyslipper to Rim Trail. I think the nest under the heather is an Oregon junco's. It managed to successfully rear the chicks right next to the trail!

Oregon Grape (*Mahonia aquifolium*)

Found only down in the Ashnola Valley and up to mid elevations. Its stunningly vivid yellow flowers bloom very early, in April or May. Later in the year, it produces masses of dark blue berries that can be made into jam. In the fall, the leaves can turn wine red or even crimson.

Black Twinberry (*Lonicera involucrate*)

A bush that grows in the sub alpine (on the Quiniscoe to Rim Trail), and produces inedible black berries . It is related to honeysuckle.

Orange Flowers

Orange Mountain Dandelion (*Agoseris aurantiaca*)

Has flower heads that can sometimes be pink or yellow, just to make life more complicated. The leaves are all basal and lance-shaped. However, the leaves in this photo are of fireweed—which was also present, though not yet in bloom.

Red Columbine
(*Aquilegia formosa*)

A very striking bloom, about a metre high. It is usually found at damp, lower elevations, but can be seen under cliffs by Pyramid Lake Trail. It prefers damp and shady areas.

Pink and Red Flowers

Western Roseroot
(*Rhodiola integrifolia*)

Also grows in the far north. It can be harvested as a green vegetable—its roots and leaves are dipped in oil and eaten by First Nations. I have seen it only a centimetre high on top of Lakeview Mountain, or as much as twenty centimetres high in lower, wetter areas.

Umbellate Pussypaws
(*Cistanthe umbellate*)

One of my favourites, found on very dry south-facing slopes, like the south side of Boxcar Mountain. It has really long, tough roots, and doesn't seem to need soil! Stems are red in colour.

Contented Alpine Wild Buckwheat (*Eriogonum pyrolifolium*)

Grows in similar locations to pussypaws. These stems are not red, and the leaves are larger. The leaves of this buckwheat are smooth and spoon-shaped, and the leafless stems are green. It can be found where the trail leaves the tree line and enters the stony ground—for example, on the Centennial Trail above Scout Lake. This is one of the drawbacks of trying to sort flowers by colour, as some flowers start off one colour and finish as another. Plants of the same genus can be many different colours.

Subalpine Wild Buckwheat (*Eriogonum umbellatum*)

Also called "sulphur buckwheat," its flowers start yellow, becoming pinker with age.

Parsnipflower Wild Buckwheat (*Eriogonum heracleoides*)

Another buckwheat variety that turns pink. These have a very noticeable whorl of leaves on the stems, with lance-shaped lower leaves.

Cushion Wild Buckwheat

Has a low white mat, with white flowers about ten centimetres high (no photo).

Indian Paintbrush (*Castilleja* species)

Another plant that is partially parasitic. There are many different types of paintbrush—some bright scarlet, some yellow or white, and some pinkish. The bright parts are usually bracts, and the actual flowers are hidden inside. It grows in open glades, and flowers from early July.

Mountain Sorrel (*Oxyria digyna*)

A striking plant that loves rocks, as long as there is a damp crack nearby. The leaves have a sharp, lemony taste, and it is a good thirst-quencher. This species is found all the way up to the Arctic, and has managed to survive through two million years of ice ages. When all the mountains were covered in ice, it survived on bleak mountaintop refugia!

Leatherleaf Saxifrage (*Leptarrena pyrofolia*)

These appear to be red even in late July. The flowers are actually white, but more often than not, you'll notice them as a mass of red stems. These pictured were around a spring, on the south side of the Boxcar.

Moss campion (*Silene acaulis*)

One of the most stunning plants, which grows into a mossy-looking mound, often on bare sand or granite. Before the flowers come out, it looks like a grassy knob. (See below.)

Orange-, Red-, and Pink-Flowered Shrubs and Berries

Pink Mountain Heather (*Phyllodoce empetriformis*)
Found all over the subalpine. Very common rock garden plant.

Bearberry (*Arctostaphylos uva-ursa*)
Otherwise known as "kinnikinnik," bearberry is found at low to mid elevations. These have bright red berries that are very mealy, but edible! The berries last right through winter.

Grouseberry (*Vaccinium scoparium*)
Produces tiny red berries that feed grouse. It comprises the major ground cover between Quiniscoe and Lake of the Woods.

Crowberry (*Emmpetrum nigrum*)

Has tiny black berries that are usually too small for humans to be bothered collecting, but which are the favourite food of ptarmigan and grouse. It is found at and above the tree line.

Soopolallie or Soapberry (*Shepherdia canadensis*)

Grows at low elevations, and is found down in the Ashnola Valley. The orange berries are very soapy and can be whipped up with sugar to make "Indian ice cream." I have used it with water to clean my oily hands after a mountain bike de-chaining!

Rosy Twisted Stalk (*Streptopus roseus*)

Grows in the damp forest at lower to mid elevations. There are three similar species, with slightly different stalk and leaf shapes. There is a healthy plant by the bridge on the trail from Pyramid to Lake of the Woods.

Common Elderberry (*Sambucus canadensis*)

The second picture is the most common elderberry colour. Grows mostly at lower elevations. There are some introduced plants between the lodge and Quiniscoe campground, probably brought up here by horses!

Purple to Blue Flowers

Fireweed (*Epilobium angustifolium*)

Not just in burnt areas, fireweed likes disturbed ground, like this patch on Diamond Trail. There are a few others in the fireweed family, such as the alpine willowherb, recognizable by its long, thin ovaries below.

Hornemann's Willowherb
(*Epilobium hornemannii*)

This willowherb is not only a different colour from its white-flowered cousin, but has broader leaves, too.

Alpine Bog Laurel
(*Kalmia microphylla*)

As its name suggests, alpine bog laurel can be found in bogs, such as along the boardwalk to Lake of the Woods. This tiny plant can also be seen around the far end of Scout Lake.

Cushion Phlox
(*Phlox pulvinata*)

These grow along the Pyramid Lake Trail to the Rim, near some white bark pine bushes. The flowers can be really pale, almost white. It blooms in mid- to late June. Sometimes it is mistaken for moss campion.

Cusick's Speedwell
(*Veronica cusickii*)

Charming little gems that grow in damper areas that get a lot of sunlight, like on the trail to Glacier Lake just above the Quiniscoe campground.

Alpine Speedwell (*Veronica wormskjoldii*) (no photo)

Has less elliptical leaves than Cusick's, and is a lighter blue with a cream centre.

Rising Suncress *(Boechera lyalli)*

Blooms in late June to August in areas recently snow-covered, high on the Rim. It is somewhat rare.

Silky Phacelia (*Phacelia serícea*)

Has leaves that are silvery and hairy, divided into numerous lobes. In the Yukon, as this plant can concentrate gold, it is being used to find gold deposits in a process called biogeochemical prospecting.

Showy Jacob's Ladder
(*Polemonium pulcherimum*)

So called because of its ladder-shaped leaves.

Showy Jacob's ladder blooming in profusion on the Lakeview Mountain Trail.

Sky Pilot *(Polemonium viscosum)*

Often amazing-looking, with bright yellow to orange centres.

Subalpine Daisy (*Erigeron glacialis*) *

Or is it an aster? Daisies and asters are best left to the experts to differenti-ate. Under the daisy flower there is one row of bracts; in asters, there are several rows, which overlap. The butterflies don't care!

Penstemon
there are over 200 species of Penstemen in North America

Very common in late May, cascading over the rocks by the Ashnola road-side. The flowers seem to spring from cracks in bare rock, and make a beautiful display. Species of penstemon are differentiated by the arrangement of their leaves around the stem or at the woody base. There is even a yellow one that grows on Mt.Kobau to the east.

Small-flowered Penstemon
(*Penstemon procerus*)

Just one of many different species of penstemons, occurring mainly in southern BC and northern Washington State.

Inky Blue Gentian
(*Gentiana glauca*)

Found around Scout Lake and there may be another species, the Northern Gentian.

Northern Gentian
(*Gentiana amarella*)

Which can be found at higher elevations than its inky blue relative. Gentians have an unmistakeable blue colour.

Lupine

There are a few species of lupine found in the park, ranging from the tiny **alpine lupine** *(Lupinus lyalli)* sometimes only a centimetre or two high, to the much larger variety found on the Pyramid Lake Trail.

There are even the occasional white ones.

Trees

Lower down in the Ashnola Valley, as in many other parts of BC, the pine beetle has run rampant and destroyed thousands of acres of forest. Most of the core area of Cathedral Park is at a higher elevation than that preferred by lodgepole pines. There are lodgepole pine (*Pinus contorta var. latifolia*) and whitebark pine (*Pinus albicaulis*), but the great majority of trees around the five lakes are—or rather, *were*—spruce (*Picea engelmannii*).

The great old stands of spruce were almost 100 percent wiped out by spruce bark beetle, and many of the pines in between were attacked by pine beetle. Only the larch (*Larix lyallii*) were left untouched. If you approach the core by the trails, the "bug kill" is not quite as noticeable as it is by the road. The giant trees, hundreds of years old, are still standing, though they've been dead since about 2005. Many have fallen down, making off-trail hiking below the lodge's elevation virtually impossible.

Rings on lodgepole pine drilled by a sapsucker (a small woodpecker).

Since all the spruce died and lost their needles, more light has entered the canopy and allowed the understorey trees to have a growth spurt. So, slowly, the forest is turning green again. Most of the younger trees are balsam (subalpine fir, *Abies lasiocarpa*).

The larch trees are all still going strong; many in Manning Park are reported to be about a thousand years old. Here in the Cathedral, we still have some very large larch

Pine-beetle-killed firewood when bucked up—shows blue stains produced by algae in the mouth parts of the pine beetle

below the trail from Ladyslipper Lake to the Rim. It would be interesting to find out their age.

Ponderosa pine bark

Lodgepole pine bark

It is simple to tell the difference. Ponderosa has three long needles, lodgepole pine has two shorter needles.

Below are pine beetle "pitch outs."

The tree tries to evict the beetles by flooding their passages with pitch. Many pine trees survive an attack by pine beetles, unlike spruce with the spruce bark beetle, which killed all the mature trees. These "pitch outs" are very characteristic of pine-beetle-killed wood, sometimes called "denim pine" or "blue pine" as a sales gimmick. The pine beetle enters the weakened tree, makes J-shaped tunnels, and then lays eggs. At high elevations, because of the cooler temperatures, the larvae grow more slowly, and live in the tree for two years instead of only one, before emerging and flying away. If there is especially cold weather early in the fall, it kills many of the larvae before they can produce their own "antifreeze," which enables them to survive until spring.

The ravages of pine beetle around Scout Lake. A few subalpine fir and pine grass supply the only greenery. The subalpine fir was not affected by the beetle attacks.

Balsam or Subalpine Fir (*Abies lasiocarpa*)

Has bark that usually has blisters, but the lower trunk loses these with age. This tree is slowly taking over around the campground areas. Unfortunately, it has shallow roots compared to spruce, and tends to blow down easily. The pitch in the blisters seems to have great healing powers on skin wounds.

Larch buds and cones (Larix lyalli).

139

In late September, as the larch start to change colour, female spruce grouse and their growing chicks are up in the larch branches, pecking. At what? Not the cones—which, I was told by a passing botanist, are only produced by the trees every fifteen years.

Golden Larch in the fall around Ladyslipper Lake. The colour change, from about September 2 into October, varies with weather!

Whitebark pine *(Pinus albicaulis)*

This pine grows right at the tree line and is the main food source of Clark's nutcrackers. They take the pinecones and bury them for future food supply, then forget where they put them! Whitebark pine is usually a smallish, bushy tree about ten metres high. They can look similar to small lodgepole pine bushes, so check for five needles instead of two. On the Quiniscoe to Rim route and the Ladyslipper Lake Trail, we have some really large whitebark pine, about twenty metres tall or higher. Human white bark pine specialists have been collecting seeds to grow more saplings, as this important tree is becoming scarce.

Engelmann Spruce *(Picea engelmannii)*

There are still two live spruces near the lodge deck—almost all the rest have died. The spruce bark beetle did not have much effect down in the valley. Many of the original spruce around the lodge were two or three times this size and up to a thousand years old! Their bark is easily recognizable, as it resembles cornflakes stuck to the trunk (though of a different colour, of course).

This specimen was found by the Ashnola River.

141

I have mentioned shrubs in relation to the colour of their flowers or berries. Juniper is usually found in "bush" form, but can also become a small tree given a suitable growing environment—as, indeed, can elderberry.

Common Juniper (*Juniperus communis var. sibirica*)

A small bush that is very common around the tree line, usually in open areas. This shrub seems to favour growing on rocks to keep warm and get more minerals and moisture. It forms a dense mat over its "host" rock, and is rarely over a metre high. The ripening dark green to ripe blue berries are medicinal for many First Nations, and are used to flavour gin. Sometimes, the needles are very sharp—not to be sat on! If the shrub grows more, the needles seem to get less sharp. Perhaps this is because they are too high to be eaten, or perhaps it is just that only new growth is prickly. Look for this stunted tree growing on and over rocks on the Quiniscoe to Rim route. Many rocks have both juniper and potentilla benefitting from the weather protection they provide.

Now, for a couple things you may spot with the trees. Though insects do not really belong in this section, the trees are where you will find them!

Cooley Spruce Adelgid

A little, aphid-like insect that lives on spruce and Douglas fir. It produces a type of gall that affects trees' buds. The larvae cause these galls to replace the growing bud. It is a hard gall and looks similar to the brown buds altered by spruce budworm, which can also eat the new bud growth. The female emerges from this gall and then goes to a Douglas fir to continue the life cycle

Spruce Budworm
Another little grub that eats new growth, then turns into a moth.

Spruce trees can survive both of these pests, as long as the infestations don't persist over a number of years. This is not the case with spruce bark beetle, which killed virtually all of the old-growth spruce in the park.

I have spent about ten years in pine beetle management, mostly around this area. I spent many weeks cutting and burning infested wood. The attempts to control the beetle were so pathetic that they verged on deliberate forest destruction. Companies took huge truckloads of infested trees to the sawmills, letting all the maturing beetles fly away to reinfect more trees. Once the trees were infected, the logging companies got them at cheaper "salvage rates." The companies at first said the beetles could only fly short distances, and preferred south-facing, mature pines. This was soon found to be false, as they blew over mountain ranges—even the Rockies. After killing the older, weaker trees they then infected smaller and smaller pine trees, and, finally, even spruce trees. Fortunately, around Princeton, the plantations contain many other tree species, so the devastation was not as complete as in, say, Prince George. Many areas around Princeton have been logged frequently, though only certain trees have been taken. As a result, we have some small patches of mixed forests. However, when I first climbed to the Rim over forty years ago, to the south, west, and north, all was forest. Now, it's a patchwork of clear-cuts and burnt areas, covered in roads and slash piles.

Logging companies in BC have been very careful over the years to ensure very few logged areas are visible from highways. Those of us that frequent the backroads know that out of sight of the highways, most of our forests have been mined almost to death. In spite of replanting, with the lack of attention and spacing during regrowth, we are left with crowded, spindly, plantations where there used to be forests. Check out some satellite photos to see what I mean!

CHAPTER 7

Mushrooms and Saprophytes

AS IS THE CASE IN all parks, visitors are reminded not to remove anything. This includes picking flowers and collecting rocks or mushrooms. Take only pictures and leave only footprints

I have been interested in mushrooms for forty years, and have collected many books on mycology. My interest began with the birth of my son: goodbye, long hikes and camp-overs; hello, short strolls with time to minutely examine the undergrowth!

"There are bold mushroom eaters, there are old mushroom eaters, but there are no old, bold mushroom eaters." I don't know who first said that, but it seems appropriate. There are at least six different types of toxins found in mushrooms, and some are deadly. Many mushroom species react badly with alcohol. Some seem to be toxic to some people, and not to others. Everyone's "gut flora" are different, so perhaps it's that some gut bacteria react badly with them. Some types can be eaten in small quantities but are toxic in larger amounts; sometimes, it is cooking them in lots of butter that causes the stomach upsets. One category of poison is similar to jet fuel, so it boils off in cooking, but can kill the cook who inhales it! No matter what, don't eat a mushroom unless you're 100 percent certain about it.

The sheer number of species and morphological varieties of fungi in BC is mind-blowing. The genus *Cortinarius*, for example, has over three thousand known species! To put that in perspective, if we were talking about a bird genus, that would mean three thousand different types of crow or three thousand different kinds of hawk! Very little is known about many mushroom varieties. Since the sixties, DNA research has shown that many fungi are not related to other, similar-looking ones. So many scientific Latin names have changed, and are still changing. It is still preferable to use them rather than common names—most fungi don't even have common names!

What we call mushrooms, fungi, or even toadstools are all only the fruiting bodies of whole organisms. The main part of a mushroom is underground or embedded in the rotting wood on which it is growing. This is usually a whitish mass of strands called the mycelium that can be found under or around the fruiting body. The mycelium converts chemicals and minerals like nitrogen and phosphorous into forms that the rootlets of plants and trees can absorb. It has been estimated that 90 percent of plants rely on mycorrhiza (the symbiosis between the fungal mycelium and the plant's roots) to help them grow to full potential. Thus, massive clear-cutting of forests or other disturbances can rid the soil of these fungal "helpers," and full growth potential is not available for years, until the mycelia are re-established.

After forest fires, with widely variable temperatures, there can be amazing amounts of morel mushrooms produced—and absolutely none in the following years. The mycelium is always there, though, unless destroyed by high-temperature fires. But it will only produce the fruiting bodies when the moisture content and temperature are correct. From down in the semi-desert of the Ashnola Valley to way up in the alpine tundra, one can come across many different types of fungi and related species. Here are some of the species most likely to be seen.

Red Lactarius (*Lactarius rufous*)

Pictured here under the spruce trees.

Rosy or Larch Bolete (*Suillus* or *Fuscoboletinus ocraceoroseus*)

Also in the image above, among the larch. At damp times of year, the number and variety of species are amazing.

Agaricus rodmanii

Down on the Ashnola Road, I have seen hundreds pushing up through the solid edges of the hard-packed gravel road, along with **Shaggy Manes (*Coprimus comatus*)** and even some **King Boletes (*Boletus edulis*)**, a popular European edible.

Leccinum insigne

Usually grow under aspen trees at lower elevations. There are a few closely related species, some of which turn dark brown or purplish upon being cut. They have sponge-like pores under the cap. They are edible, but not very tasty!

Suillus Cavipes

It has a hollow stalk, and grows only under larch trees.

Suillus Lakeii

This *suillus* grows on the "Sage Ridge" on the Lakeview Trail into the core area. It stains brown with handling. It is very similar to other *Suillus* species, like **Suillus brevipes** (*brevipes* means "short-stalk") and **Suillus cavipes** (above), though these do not stain on handling and are different shades of yellowish. These are all good edibles.

King Bolete, Steinpiltz, or Porcini (*Boletus edulis*)

This specimen was found in the Ashnola. Sometimes they show up on the ridge above Glacier Lake, but weather conditions, including moisture and temperature, have to be just right.

Fungi come in an amazing variety of sizes, colours, and make-up. There are the "classic" mushroom shapes, with a stalk and a cap (*Tricholomas*), some with gills under the cap, some with pores or holes. Some even have spines underneath (*Hydnacae*). Some have short, wide gills, and some have "decurrent" gills that continue down the stem. Other types have internal spaces in which their spores are produced; some look like wall brackets, some like cauliflowers, and some like footballs. Some even look like tiny bird nests with eggs. During damp fall days, vast groups of tiny *Mycena* species emerge from the rotting woody debris, little white caps only millimetres across.

Toward Identification

The families of fungi are classified by all these differences. *Boletes* and *Suillus* families are "mushroom-shaped" and have pores (tiny holes the spores fall out of) under the cap. Amanitas all spring from a universal veil or vulva that looks like a puffball at first; as the mushroom grows, the remains of the veil often leave white blotches on the caps.

In addition to gilled mushrooms, there are many other families: puffballs, jelly fungus, morels, cup fungi, truffles, spine fungi, corals and clubs, polypores, and probably many more!

What is it?   *Making a spore print*

The first step in identification is to make a spore print. Place the mushroom cap spore-surface-down on a pale-coloured surface. If the mushroom has white spores, you may not be able to see them, though, so sometimes I put the cap half on a pale surface, half on a dark surface. After leaving it overnight, you usually get a spore print. This chocolate brown spore print identifies an Agaricus. From the first impression, it's difficult to identify. When you see the pink to chocolate brown gills and a ring is visible, it becomes clear it is *Agaricus campestris,* one of the more common edible mushrooms, similar to what you'd find in a grocery store.

More Gilled Mushrooms Examples

First, check the gill attachment. Are the gills waxy? Check the spore colour. Does it have a ring? Is the cap sticky?

Gomphidius glutinosus

Gomphidius are also called "peg-tops," because when they first emerge they look like pegs. These have a sticky cap, usually; hence, the *glutinosus* in the name. The yellow colour from its base to its stalk makes it easy to recognize. They have decurrent gills—i.e., going down the stalk. They grow near conifers.

Below, you will find some genus characteristics. Once you have the genus, use a good book to try and find the species. Good luck!

Russulas

The stalks of Russulas snap like a stick of chalk. The Russulas can be different colours, from bright red to pink, orange, and yellow. They have close gills underneath. One species is **Russula emetica**. These are often bright

red, though they get to be a pale pink after rain washes out their colour. The Latin *emetica* means they will make you throw up.

Lactarius

The Lactarius family are identified by white spore print, but more easily by running your fingernail across the gills. The line you made will produce milky fluid (hence "lactarius"). If it's blood red, it's probably **Lactarius rufous**. If carrot-coloured, it's probably **Lactarius deliciosus**.

Amanitas

Fairly easily identifiable because they grow out of a volva in the ground that often leaves white pieces on top of the cap.

The stem also has a ring, and the spore print is usually white. In the high alpine near Twin Buttes, I have found very large specimens up to thirty centimetres in diameter. Almost all Amanitas are poisonous, and some are deadly. Common names are "Destroying Angel" and "Death Cap"!

Amanitra pantherina are poisonous (deadly), and quite common on Diamond Trail in the fall.

Fly agaric (*Amanita muscaria*) is usually red-capped, but not always. It can vary a lot in colour.

Old and soggy Amanitas, still with white veil remnants on the caps

The classic poison mushroom (Amanita muscaria)

Pholiota

There are a few different species—some are edible and some are poisonous. Usually, they grow on the base of old or dead fir and spruce in late August or September. They are very scaly on both cap and stalk below ring.

Tricholoma

This species used to be called **Armillaria**. The same genus as the more famous pine mushroom (matsutake), this one is not edible. It feels very solid, and has a white ring and white spore print.

Hygrophorus

Hygrophorus speciosus is just one of the Hygrophorus family, the larch waxy cap. These are usually small and brightly coloured, but they have thin flesh, waxy-feeling gills, and no ring. There are about 200 species, but they are not easily identifiable. This one is usually found under larch in boggy areas.

Strophariaceae

The Stropharia family contains some hallucinogenic mushrooms. They have purple to brown spore prints and a ring on the stalk. The stalk is scaly below the ring. **Stropharia hornemanii** (top) and slightly stockier **Stropharia ambigua** (below) can be found in the spruce/subalpine fir zone on the Lake of the Woods Trail.

Laccaria

The most commonly seen species of this genus is Laccaria bicolour, which is bright orange. Others are often purplish.

Laccaria bicolor

This is a very bright orange mushroom common around Quiniscoe. It has a white spore print, slightly purplish gills, and flutings down the stalk. The cap looks velvety. There are others in the Laccaria genus that are more purple, and some are paler— Laccaria laccata, for example.

Hydnacae

Hydnellum auriantiacum

A kind of spine fungus. The underside of the cap has tiny spines on which the spores are produced. Some spine fungi are edible when young and fresh.

Hydnum imbricatum

Another species of Hydnum (with spore-producing spines underneath the cap). It is paler when fresh, becoming darker brown later. These can get to be really huge—about thirty centimetres across—and look like old, rotten logs.

Pig's ears (*Discina perlata*)

I found these on the Goat Lake Trail. They are about five centimetres across and they have no stipe (stalk.) The undersurface produces the spores.

The top view   *The spore producing underside*

The Ramaria genus

has many hundreds of species, but the only ones you may see in Cathedrals are probably Ramaria abietina growing on the ground in groves of trees. They can grow to be thirty centimetres across, and are supposedly edible, but I've never tried! **Ramaria mag-nipes** is mostly below ground, the above-ground part looking like a head of cauliflower.

Checking my find (on the left) against the illustration in one of my mushroom books,
Mushrooms of Western Canada *by Helene M. E. Schalkwijk-Barendsen.*
All the illustrations are hand-painted. Often in earlier "mushroom" books, the photographic
colours did not do justice to the actual colour. That is why paintings can often look more
accurate than a photograph.

Clavariadelphus sachalinensis

Otherwise known as earth tongues, or sometimes "dead man's fingers"! I
found thousands of these purple ones called **Clavaria purpurea** down the
hillside below Stone City.

These species vary somewhat in size, from a few millimetres to about
twelve centimetres.

Puffballs (*Calvatia*, *Lycoperdon*, and more)

These occur in many shapes and sizes; all are edible while white inside, but soon they "ripen" into a skin full of brown, dusty spores. Make sure they are not young, poisonous "amanitas"—always cut them in half to see.

Hooded False Morel (*Gyromitra infusa*)

These are sometimes mistaken for morels, but beware, they are poisonous! I have never found edible morels in the Cathedrals. There was just one at Lake of the Woods in July 2019, but following recent forest fires there may be some Morchella elata or angusticeps showing up soon!

Gyromitra Montana

These grow at high elevations, usually in early summer. A distant relative to morels, they are considered edible.

Pycnoporellus alboluteus

This brilliant orange fungi grows on rotting spruce logs and has no common name.

Polypores

This family comes in many different shapes and sizes. The commonest are the "conks"—hard, shelf-like growths on trees—but some polypores have stalks and grow on buried wood on the ground. The characteristic they have in common is that the spores are produced from really tiny holes under the cap.

Heterobasidion annosum looks like **Fomitopsis pinicola**, but doesn't have any red colouration. Both cause brown rot in the base of conifer trees. They are very common but too hard to attempt to eat!

Here is a strange one!

It's a polypore; it has stipes and off-centre caps that meld together. It gives a white spore print, and the creamy, soft flesh doesn't stain. I think it is "Bondarzew's" Polypore," or maybe Albatrellus (*Polyporus montanus*) but none of my books convinced me.

Saprophytes

These look like plants, but behave like fungi, as they have no green chlorophyll to turn sunlight into energy through conversion into sugars. Instead, they take their nourishment from the roots of nearby plants, and in return, they break down minerals in the soil that the plants can use.

Pine Drops (*Pterospora andromode*)

Orange-coloured when new, these are dark brown if you find them in early spring, sticking up through the snow.

There are other saprophytes, such as coralroots, although I have never found them in the park. They are recognizable by their total lack of green parts, and they have yellow or brown rather than green stems.

There are so many amazing species that the more you learn, the more you are amazed! Although it's now over forty years since I walked with my toddler through fields of mushrooms, my interest is still there, and fungi remain as fascinating as ever! Now I am an old, almost bold mushroom-eater, as I can recognize sufficient species to get by!

CHAPTER 8

Mammals, Birds, Snakes, and the Tracks They Make

BACK WHEN I WAS A kid in Stockport, there was no such thing as wildlife, except when the pub closed! We would take a bus out to Lyme Park, and look for squirrels leaping from branch to branch over the road. If you hiked for an hour or two, you might glimpse, in the distance, a couple of red deer of the park's herd. Spotting other wildlife was very unlikely. I spent most of my spare time in Woodbank Park, by the smelly river Goyt. I don't remember ever seeing any wildlife other than birds. The river was so polluted from the cloth-dyeing factories and cotton mills upstream that it would be blue or red or grey on different days! In summer, you could smell the river from a mile away!

Here are just some the species observed in Cathedral Park—dependent, of course, on the season and the habitat: black bear, mountain sheep, mountain goat, mule deer, moose, cougar, lynx, wolf, coyote, hoary marmot, yellow-bellied marmot, pine chipmunk, pica, porcupine, otter, Columbian ground squirrel, golden-mantled ground squirrel, least weasel, pine marten, fox, many types of vole, mouse, and shrew, and, possibly, grizzly bear, fisher, wolverine, and bobcat. Now, you wouldn't see any of that back in Lyme Park!

I took all the photographs in this book, but I haven't been lucky enough to see and photograph all the species. Fauna includes birds, of course, such as Clark's nutcrackers, grey jays, ptarmigans, grouse, hawks, owls, spotted sandpipers, common loons, and many more (see appendix for the bird list). Many of the animals around the two campgrounds in the core area are very used to humans and appear quite tame. This is partly because dogs are not allowed, and humans have not been threatening. However, animals (young hares or chipmunks, for example) should not be picked up or fed. This includes various kinds of mice, squirrels, marmots, ground squirrels, chipmunks, deer, goats, and so on.

Unlike hares and weasels, who change to white coats in winter, goats are always white— unless they're having a dust bath!

Mountain Goat (*Oreamnos americanus*)

From grassy valley floors to rocky peaks, from snow fields to campsites, goats are where you find them! They roam all over the park. Sometimes they are with others or sometimes all alone, halfway up a cliff. Can you see a white spot up on the cliff? Check it out with your binoculars! Goats can be in amazing places, looking for nourishment.

In 2018, BC Parks decided that very little was known about the habits of the goats, who sometimes disappear for a couple of weeks at a time. Eight rangers and helpers came up to try and put collars on some goats in order to track their movements. The goats must have hacked into all the e-mails, because they promptly disappeared for two weeks. In 2019, the procedure was repeated, with more success. Ten goats were collared, using either tranquilizer darts or a "clover trap" with a salt block bait. Six females and four males were weighed, measured, and collared. Collars numbered 1, 2, 3, 4, 9, and 10 were females, and numbers 7, 8, 11, and 18 were males. See if you can tell them apart! The horns are shaped a little differently. If they have a gradual curve and the bases are larger, they're probably male; if the horn has a sharper curve and there is a wider space between the horn bases, they're probably female. It's a lot easier to tell them apart when they lose their heavy winter coats.

Sometimes, there are as many as twenty-five goats walking around the campgrounds. The kids tend to stay closer to mother, but not always. They like to chase each other around the group. So, keep those guy lines high so they don't run into them!

Setting up the "clover trap": the bait is the blue salt lick used for cattle. Even after the salt was removed, goats licked the ground until there was a trench twenty centimetres deep and a metre long!

Bighorn sheep (*Ovis canadensis*)

In early spring, bighorn sheep can be seen around the junction of the Ashnola and Similkameen Valleys. When the snow is gone, they move back up the mountains—but not often into the Cathedral core area. There are herds on Crater Mountain and also around Sheep Station in the Snowy Mountain Wilderness Area (see Chapter 5). In winter, they can often be seen down in the bottom of the Similkameen.

Recently, the herds picked up a kind of mite that attacked their ears, eventually deafening them. This made them easy prey for cougars, wolves, and even coyotes. A few years before that, there was a big die-off from

165

tuberculosis. The disease was caught from domestic sheep, I believe, but the wild sheep made a comeback. Their habitat gets lessened every year by human activity, and limits their ability to meet other herds and interbreed, and thus they become more threatened.

Mule Deer (*Odocoileus hemionus*)

Mule deer are very common around the lodge area and Lake of the Woods. They know they are protected here! In the fall, they go lower down the mountain, and once outside the core area, they can be hunted. I hope they don't stand and stare at the hunters like they do up here. These photographs weren't taken with a telephoto—they're as close as they look. Their winter coat is grey and thicker but they lose this and become browner for the summer. The bucks lose their antlers every year and grow new ones. The old ones are found and chewed on by wolves and coyotes in the winter.

Recently, someone told me they had seen elk at Glacier Lake, and they showed me the photos on their cameras. The pictures were only very big male mule deer with huge racks. I have seen moose scat around the core area, but no elk yet!

Moose scat and print.

Snowshoe Hare (*Lepus americanus*)

Snowshoe hares are so cute when small, and are often seen around Quiniscoe Campground. They only survive about three years. Females sometimes have two litters of one to five leverets per year. They will provide food for the rest of the food chain. The diet of Lynx is 96 percent snowshoe hare!

Ooh! Fresh shoots!

The snowshoe hares become white in winter, as do weasels, which become ermine. The pelage change is brought about by the shortening and lengthening of the days as winter comes and goes. Sometimes, the weather is a little out of step with the length of the day, and you get white hares on brown ground or brown hares on white snow! In the spring (early June up here), there are brown hares with white socks on.

River Otter (*Lutra canadensis*)

I know this isn't a great photo, but let me tell you a story. One day, I decided to see if I could hike over the Boxcar to the Haystacks Lakes and back before cleaning the outhouses and collecting fees before dark. Going at a great pace, I managed to reach the basalt block summit of Haystack Mountain by 11:30 a.m. I then hiked down the ridge and around the cliff to what looked like a tropical paradise, a turquoise-blue lake, a white sandy beach under a blazing sunny, blue sky. Doffing my clothes, I decided a quick dip was in order. No sooner had I entered the water than a loud barking noise over my shoulder surprised me. Turning around, I was amazed to see two otters telling me to get out of their lake! Not being a great swimmer and valuing my tender flesh, I beat a hasty retreat to the beach. It was tempting to stay a few days, but I had to return, almost at a trot, back the way I had come. I made it to camp at about 5 p.m. and managed to do the rounds before dark—a wonderful if exhausting day!

The remoteness and elevation of Haystacks Lake indicate that the otters must have walked miles, as had I, but I guess their need for fish was greater than mine. They deserved to fish there.

Ground Squirrel (*Citellus columbianus*)

Is this the rare two-headed ground squirrel? Or is it just a cautious young-ster? These animals are a great favourite with visitors, especially when they pop up almost under your feet and run squeaking to vanish down the nearest tunnel. You can see them on the Glacier Lake Trail. If you stay absolutely still, they may come back out again to check you out! And if it is safe, they bring up their kids!

Golden-Mantled Ground Squirrel (*Citellus lateralis*)

Apparently, these animals used to be fairly common around the lodge in earlier days; however, the yellow-bellied marmots took over their habitat. In the last few years, they have made a huge comeback. They are all over the place, especially around the lodge—even in your luggage, if you aren't careful! Some are very tame, because they are hand-fed around the lodge. Feeding animals is not allowed in the park, because it can be dangerous.

And what are the animals meant to eat once the tourists have gone, if they've grown habituated to human food?

Yellow-Bellied Marmot (*Marmota flaviventris*)

Yellow-bellied marmots are often seen lazing around in the sun on the rocks at the Quiniscoe campsite. They must be much smarter than humans—they spend nine months of the year sleeping and socializing underground, and the rest sunbathing on the rocks! These are considerably larger than Columbian ground  squirrels, which are about thirty centimetres long, including the tail. Marmots are about fifty centimetres long, and quite fat and heavy-looking in the summer.

Hoary Marmots (*Marmota caligata*)

These are a little bigger than their yellow-bellied cousins. They range higher up on the Rim, in among the rugged rocks. There are a few hoary marmots lower down, at the end of Quiniscoe Lake. Their faces are noticeably blacker and their upper backs are grey, just like a silver back gorilla or an old grizzly bear. They will sit on a high boulder and whistle when you approach (did you know that was how Whistler Resort got its name?). So, at a glance, if it looks black and grey and big, then it's a hoary; if it's smaller, brown, and golden-bellied, it's a yellow-bellied!

Pika (*Ochotona princeps*)

It is pronounced *pie-ka* by most people, *pee-ka* by others. But you say tomatoe, I say tomahto. Pica are usually seen up among the rocks on the talus slopes, storing hay for the coming winter. Their high-pitched squeak will alert you to the fact that you have been seen entering their rocky terrain. They will squeak loudly, but they are not always easily seen, as they blend in so well. They are quite small—only about fifteen centimetres long, with no tail.

You may see their little piles of hay half-hidden in the rocks. Once the hay is dried, they hide it deeper in the rocks to last them through the long, cold winter. Pika are quite common up in the rock piles between the alpine larch and the tundra of the alpine in this park, but are becoming scarce in other parts of the continent. Global climate change narrows the ecological zone in which they can live. It lessens every year as the tree line elevation slowly rises but the actual mountains don't. Pikas don't actually hibernate, but keep active under the snow. In early October, with a foot of snow on the ground, the pikas were still shouting at me as I trudged by.

Pikas' winter haystack storage under the rocks.

Yellow Pine Chipmunk (*Eutamias amoenus*)

There are at least seven different species of chipmunk in North America, but this is the only species in Cathedral Park. They are tiny (113-132 millimetres long), dark-brown-and-tan-striped blurs running across your campsite, occasionally stopping to look at you before rushing off again to look for food. Chipmunks will steal all your food if you let them—even from sealed packs! So hang up all your food. In fact, hang up even non-food items such as hand creams, toothpaste, and so on.

Red Squirrel (*Tamiasciurus hudsonicus*)

In summer, the black line along the sides of a red squirrel's white belly are very prominent. Red squirrels often pick up pieces of fungi and then store them for winter, as they do with pinecones. They bury pine or fir-cones under the duff, and often forget where they've put them. To save fungi as a food source, they carry them up into the branches and leave them to dry for winter. Just because a squirrel eats it doesn't necessarily mean it's fit for human consumption!

Go big and go home! Our friend tries to take a large larch bolete, to his winter storage

A squirrel at Lake of the Woods collected all these for the coming winter!

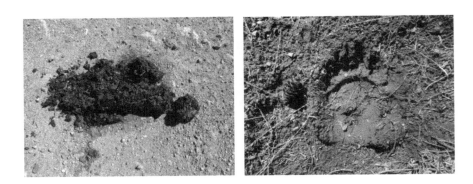

This is bear scat found in the valley on the Ashnola Road—during berry season, obviously! If a person can hike up in a day, then so can a bear. So keep your campsite clean, with no food available for wandering bears. A fed bear is a dead bear.

Canadian lynx (*Felis lynx*)

I managed to get this photo by placing a "stealthcam" on a game trail near my cabin. All I got for a few nights were pictures of nocturnal mice running around in the dark. Lynx are around, but you never see them! I once found a dead one near Lake of the Woods. About 96 percent of the lynx's diet is snowshoe hare, so if there are lots of hares, there are lynx around. The hare population crashes every few years, closely followed by the lynx population.

Northern Pacific Rattlesnake (*Crotalus oreganus oreganus*)

Down in the valley, you can encounter rattlesnakes. Please try and avoid them while driving! They are very wary and will quickly disappear, if possible, when they feel footstep vibrations on the ground. I found one that had its head totally squashed flat by a car, yet was still rattling its tail to an uncaring world. Being cold-blooded, they have to cool down before they are really dead.

Tracks

*Because dogs are not allowed in the park,
new snowfalls can leave stories*

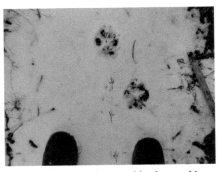

A wolf and a robin sized bird passed by.

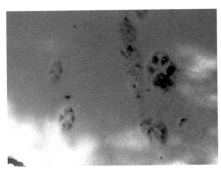

*A wolf and a fox were going the same
direction—presumably at different times!*

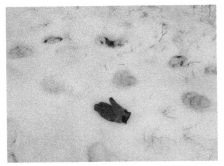

*Cougar and lynx tracks can be seen in early
snowfalls—even a bear walking around
Lake of the Woods.*

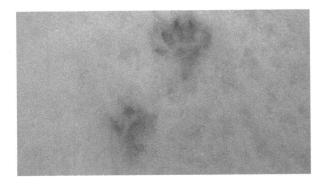

A pine marten track (five toes means weasel family) found near Smokey the Bear.

Birds

Birds provide another excellent reason to visit Cathedral Provincial Park. This book does not set out to name them all, just to familiarize the reader and visitor with the more common species. Many people now have bird-song apps on their phones to make identification easier. I still don't even have a phone! In the appendix is a fairly recent list of all the species found in Cathedral Park. Featured are those I've managed to photograph while working and walking in the park. There are many "LBJ's" (little brown jobs) that are gone as soon as you get your binoculars out! Don't even think about trying to photograph them! I can recognize the songs of some of them—Swainson's thrush, Pacific wren, robins, varied thrush, juncos, and so on. I prefer to identify birds visually, if I can. So I always carry binoculars, and have a bird book handy.

Spruce Grouse (*Falcipennis canadensis*)

The male spruce grouse, otherwise known as "Franklin's grouse."

You can almost trip over them on the trails. Often, a surprised mother with chicks softly croons and clucks, telling them not to move. A hen starts with perhaps eight chicks, but can be down to only one by the end of September. They feed a lot of other animals!

Immature spruce grouse.

Adult female.

Above the tree line, ptarmigan are found. Mostly white-tailed, though some are possibly rock ptarmigan (Lagopus muta).

White-tailed Ptarmigan (Lagopus leucura)

Ptarmigan chicks are so well-camouflaged that they are almost impossible to see amongst the rocks on the Rim. Can you see the chick below?

These are amazing birds, out on the highest peaks in all weather.

This one is turning white for the winter!

Horned Larks (*Eremophila alpestris*)

On the tundra—for example, on the Rim Trail—flocks of birds can be seen swooping from one place to another close by. These are often horned larks—look for a crest and black chest markings.

Grey-crowned Rosy Finch (*Leucosticte tephrocotis*)

Sometimes, later in the summer, flocks of grey-crowned rosy finches can be sighted. This species has a couple of sub-species, and they range from the Alaskan Islands as far south as Washington. They seem to move constantly, and are very difficult to photograph without a very good camera with a telephoto lens—and a lot of patience!

Osprey (*Pandion haliaetus*)

This photo was taken at a grassland area near Merritt, but we often get osprey around the lakes. They don't seem to nest up in the core area, but they are frequent visitors. They are often seen squabbling with bald eagles over fishing rights. If you get to view them from below, check out the black feathers around their "elbows"—a good identifier.

Sandhill Cranes (*Grus canadensis*)

Occasionally, if you are lucky, you can hear a really unmistakeable call, described as "trumpeting"—a faraway sound that almost makes the hair on the back of your neck stand up. If you scan the skies, you may see, a thousand metres above your head, a flock of sandhill cranes.

I have seen these magnificent birds circle right over Grimface Mountain, gaining elevation in spirals, until they are mere dots in the sky, still trumpeting. Over 3,000 metres up, they fly south to Texas for the coming winter. I saw twenty-five of them on September 21, 2020.

Sandhill cranes (dots in the sky).

American Three-toed Woodpecker (*Picoides dorsalis*)

This is the female. They have a black-and-white-barred back, and the males have a yellow flash on the top of their heads. If the back is solidly black, then it is probably a black-backed woodpecker (*Picoides arctius*) instead. They all love flinging huge chunks of bark off the dead spruce as they look for insect larvae. Also present in the park are the gorgeous pileated woodpeckers (*Dryocopus pileatus*). These look huge by comparison. They have a very obvious red crest. I have heard their calls but never seen them here

Grey Jay or Whiskey Jack (*Perisorius canadensis*)

This bird can be very noisy—and very nosey! They can make all kinds of strange noises, and love to come and see what you are doing. You can be totally alone on an alpine peak when one will appear, soon to be joined by others, looking for handouts. Please don't feed them! Clark's nutcrackers can behave the same way—very noisily! Remember to compare the beaks—large for nutcrackers, small for whiskey jacks.

Clark's Nutcracker (*Nucifraga columbiana*)

This cheeky fellow was trying to get through my window to steal things off the windowsill! Look at the size of the nutcracking beak!

Common Loon (*Gavia immer*)

Occasionally, the easily-recognized loon call echoes around Quiniscoe Lake. They don't seem to nest here, but one or two sometimes hang around for a couple of days.

Sometimes a pair of garganeys or Barrow's goldeneye (Bucephala islandica) *will visit, but only the Barrow's have nested up here, down by the west end of Quiniscoe Lake.*

The nest—more of a depression—I found belonging to a spotted sandpiper (Actitis macularius).

Sandpipers give away the nest location by making such a commotion as you pass by. They started nesting here about four years ago and now there are a few every year. They constantly jerk up and down as they search for food by the shoreline.

Butterflies

Brushfoot genus, fritillary family

There are six main families of butterflies in North America, and each family has a number of subgroups. So, start by identifying which family a butterfly belongs to and go from there—but don't forget to sit and watch and enjoy. It is not always necessary to *do*—just to be! Once again, I would recommend buying a good book if you are keen on butterfly identification. Not unlike mushrooms, there are so many different types it boggles the mind. It is quite possible, as with mushrooms, that there may be a few undiscovered or undescribed species out there!

The six families are Swallowtails, whites and yellows, gossamer-wings, metalmarks, brush-foots, and skippers. These amazing insects are found in a wide variety of different environments—often, because of the very specific plants they eat as food (i.e., the plants' nectar), both for themselves and the leaves for their caterpillars. If you find a certain type of vegetation, then you may find a particular butterfly species. The advantage of butterfly-spotting over birding, I've been told, is that you don't have to get up at dawn!

Brushfoots (*Nymphalidae*) are the family of butterflies that is probably the most common in the core area. Their favourite plants seem to be asters and thistles. In this family are many species, such as fritillaries, which themselves come in a few different forms. It is very difficult to tell them apart unless you actually have a dead specimen in good condition in your hand.

Mourning cloak (Nymphalis antiopa) *is a very dark kind of brush-foot, quite common at lower elevations*

Gossamer-wings (Lycaenidae) *are another butterfly family, with four genera and many species. These may be "Silvery Blues" or "Arrowhead Blues", whose favourite pollen source is lupines.*

Another gossamer-wing

Swallowtails also includes Parnassians, like these Phoebus parnassian (Parnassian phoebus)

These parnassians can be seen at high elevations, flying low to the ground, even during a snowstorm! Stonecrops are the favourite food for their caterpillars. This beautiful butterfly has brilliant red dots on the wings. Close up, you can see that the males have antennae with black and white rings around them. The females have darker, trailing wing edges. Western tiger swallowtails occur down in the valley, along with many other species.

Small tortoiseshell (Nymphalis urtica) *getting the nectar from moss campion near the summit of Lakeview mountain*

I am fairly new to observing butterflies. As a kid, we seldom saw them due to air pollution in the industrial north of England. I always remember a holiday our family took to a farmhouse on the Llyn peninsula of North Wales, where, as a twelve-year-old, I was amazed at the numbers of brilliant butterflies.

I would not be surprised if there are many species up in the core area just waiting to be discovered, as there seems to be few people around with the expertise.

A few years ago, my wife and I found millions of monarch butterflies resting in south Texas before continuing their migration to the mountains of Mexico.

CHAPTER 9

Fishing

IT WAS TIP ANDERSON WHO told me that Pat Parson's granddad (the man who founded Parsons Fruit Stand in Keremeos) and another fellow (Herb Clark) had brought a packhorse up to Cathedral Lakes with tea chests full of trout fry lashed to each side of the horse. They had to keep topping up the water, as so much was spilled on the way up. Well, that's Tip's story. Could even be true! I think they used helicopters later!

Quiniscoe Lake. Red-coated fisherman seeking fish and solitude

Of the five lakes in the core area, Quiniscoe, Lake of the Woods, Pyramid, and Ladyslipper all have good to great fishing for trout—both cutthroat and rainbow. However, I have fished in Glacier Lake, but never caught anything. Walking around the lake on numerous occasions, I have never seen any fish rise or seen fish close to shore, as you can at Ladyslipper. Occasionally, a duck or two might appear, but I really think there are no fish in it, and very little other life (though there are leeches!)

A colourful cutthroat from Ladyslipper Lake

In early June, as the snow melt continues, many spawning trout leave Quiniscoe Lake and enter the small creeks that leave the lake at the east end (near the lodge). Sometimes, hundreds of spawning fish can be seen in the shallow pools, where they are very visible and unprotected from the predations of bald eagles and ospreys. I have seen a bald eagle fight with an osprey for its dinner right on the footbridge. If you happen to come up in early June, be aware that this is a very sensitive area. Don't let your kids wade around in the creek! By the end of June, the water level drops about thirty centimetres, and the trout all return to the lake. Small fry from two to ten centimetres to inhabit the shallow pools continuously, year-round. In very high water, I have even seen trout stuck in the bushes surrounding the creek. I think they lose their way in the strong currents.

A similar scenario unfolds at Lake of the Woods, where lots of trout leave the lake to spawn in the tiny, shallow exit stream. I have seen eagles sitting on the footbridge and plunging in to grab a fish. It's just too easy! From scat on the bridge, it is evident that otters and other animals try the same tricks.

The trout populations in all the lakes seem to stay fairly consistent, and they are no longer stocked. Way back in 1964, I think, they were stocked with rainbow and cutthroat. Apparently, Ladyslipper Lake and Haystacks Lake also had California golden trout introduced. So the old tale about golden trout in the fall in Haystacks Lakes is probably based in fact. Many of the fish from Ladyslipper can look like hybrids of all three species.

Quiniscoe Lake

With a maximum depth of twelve metres, this lake is fished the most, due to the proximity of the campground and lodge, and the use of canoes and boats. There always seems to be some action—especially with dry flies. I have had success with all kinds of flies, but if you are just trying to catch a trout for supper, then a "tom thumb" or something similar will usually work. The end of the lake closest to the lodge is very shallow, and by the end of September, many rocks and sunken trees are visible. The best place to fish is toward the waterfall end, from rocks on either side of the deeper water—or, of course, you can rent a canoe from the lodge.

Lake of the Woods

With a maximum depth of 3.6 metres, this beautiful lake is an easy twenty-minute walk from Quiniscoe. Here, the fish tend to only be fifteen to twenty centimetres long, but are very plentiful. This lake is shallow, and I really wonder how the fish manage in winter, as it can drop to minus-forty up here. Does the lake freeze solid, or is it insulated by the deep snow-pack—about a metre and a half?

On very warm summer days, the fish try to stay at the shady end or in the reeds. Sometimes, they are in such a feeding frenzy, the whole surface of the lake erupts with fish, as if they are trying to escape!

Pyramid Lake

Looking south across Pyramid Lake from the shallow north end

Pyramid Lake is an easy ten-minute walk from Quiniscoe. This lake, with a maximum depth of 7.2 metres, has some larger fish, especially out toward the far end. Pyramid is very shallow at the exit creek and along the north side. The deepest area is below the jumbled rock slide on the south side.

Ladyslipper Lake

Ladyslipper is the deepest—twelve metres at least. It takes most people at least an hour to hike up and over the ridge to this gorgeous blue gem. There are many cutthroat and rainbow trout in this lake, but they seem to be a bit more wary than those at Lake of the Woods or Pyramid. They are often of a much larger size, which may compensate

the fisherman for the effort of getting here! A red and white spoon lure has worked really well here, especially in September.

Around July 20, fish look for areas of finer gravels in which to lay their eggs and cover them for protection. So many edges of the lake are just not suitable, with large, immovable, sharp-edged rocks. I think some fish spawn a little lower in the creek, but it drops so steeply from the lake that it can't be far—or the newly hatched young would never make it back against the current.

Pairs of spawning fish are to be seen in the shallow edges of the lake and at the far end, where the little creek exits.

Goat Lake

Goat Lake is about a ninety-minute hike from Quiniscoe, and only has a few small trout. The deeper areas are best, on the side opposite the trail. A pair of otters was seen fishing there in 2023, so there may not be many fish left in the lake! There are also many small trout in the creek beside the trail.

Goat Lake from the top of the Boxcar.

Scout Lake and Mountain Goat Lakes

Neither of these lakes has any fish, as they are both very shallow and may freeze solid.

Haystacks Lake

If you feel ambitious and have the time and camping equipment, you might consider hiking over. There are certainly lots of trout in the main lake. It is well worth the trip for the scenery alone, but it is a long way off! The lakes are full of fish. I caught five on five casts in five minutes the last time I was there! Only one of the lakes is deep enough to support trout—the others are very shallow and almost dry up at the end of summer. The distance to Haystacks is probably too far for most people to return in one day, but it has been done!

Finally, down below the core area in the Ashnola Valley, there are many beautiful fishing holes, which mostly yield small rainbows. Due to spring run-off, the river frequently changes. This year's pool may be next year's beaver dam, or even a dry channel—especially upstream, where the valley widens out. The lower canyon, below the Horseshoe campgrounds, has some great pools.

Fishing, like camping, should always be no-trace. Please ensure you don't leave pieces of line or other garbage. If you're keeping your catch, clean it a long way from both the water and your tent site, and treat the remains like any other garbage—i.e., bag it and take it home.

The Ashnola River has many quiet reaches that are great fishing, but see the hung-up log? The spring flood left it!

This is the same river in early June, travelling about ninety kilometres an hour! The spring floods are awesome and I wonder how any fish manage to stay in the upper river

This scene was caught on Vancouver Island. The perils of fishing! I don't think this has ever happened in this park. When in doubt, throw it back!

EPILOGUE

ON THE FIFTEENTH OF AUGUST, 2023, I woke up with a very sore throat, with my eyes all plugged up. I had a quick wash in water from the lake, as the spring that supplies the cabin had already dried up. After a few hours of work cleaning the outhouses and so on, I decided that I was too sick to work and started to make arrangements to leave, a day before my seven-day shift was over.

As I drove down the road in the early afternoon, I saw that the wildfire to the south had really grown and was producing a lot of smoke. Another wildfire to the north on the flanks of Crater Mountain was also growing.

That evening, from on my deck in Princeton, I could see a huge mushroom cloud of smoke, a pyrocumulous billowing skywards, already probably over three thousand metres high. Later, on the local news, I heard that the two fires had joined up. The next evening, from my deck again, I saw an even larger pyrocumulous, shot through with red streaks, turning gold then purple in the setting sun.

Well! I thought, *there goes Cathedral Park!* With all the dead old spruce in the valley and dead pines higher up, I felt sure the park would be totally destroyed.

A few days later, at home recovering from my eye infection, I found out what had happened. Maybe it wouldn't be as bad as I feared. Most importantly, I learned, no lives were lost.

The fire from forty kilometres away!

The day after I left Cathedral Park, an evacuation alert was given, and all the lodge guests and campers were notified. They all spent an uneasy night before being evacuated by road the following morning. Later, the fire ravaged the basecamp, burning the bridge and housing before flying up the valley toward the lodge and core area. The huge amounts of fuel available from the dead spruce and pine made a very intense fire that totally destroyed much of the forest. The fire roared up the valley, consuming everything in its path until it reached the top of the hill at the lodge clearing. Then, it stopped!

A clear line extended from the top of the lodge's upper parking lot across the end of the lake to the edge of the Quiniscoe campground. All of the lodge buildings, the parks cabin on the other side of the lake, and the Quiniscoe campground were all saved. Only one outhouse was lost! Amazing but true. A few embers, blown by the wind, fell in the campground and started spot fires. Thankfully, these fires only burnt little patches of a few square metres before going out.

Forest fires vary tremendously in heat and intensity. Some soils will be left totally sterile, or may erode away with spring run-off. Other sites may have had only enough heat to melt the resin in old pinecones sufficient to start germination and regrowth. Some species, like fireweed, will quickly take over in spring; there may be morels in damper areas. Seeds and berries, buried by squirrels and nutcrackers, will start to grow, and a different and wonderful natural landscape will reveal itself.

Fire is essentially a natural process, and this particular one had been artificially delayed for a long time.

The immediate future of the park and lodge is uncertain at this time. BC Parks may not have the manpower or feel it to be a priority to clear the trails of danger trees and deadfall. It follows that the park facilities have changed considerably since the fire, so not all the information given regarding trails and camping, number of outhouses, and so on is still accurate.

To my knowledge, at least nine outhouses will need replacing, a few were burnt and others are too old. Probably, two campgrounds will need re- planning, and at the moment there are only thirty tent-sites available, in the Core Area at Quiniscoe. Numbers of visitors will have to be severely limited to the available facilities, and, most importantly for the operators of the park, no money will be made. Who will pay to have a park facility operator up there? I don't really want to retire yet but . . . to be continued.

Some things are certain, The mountains will remain in place, and Nature will reclothe the barren slopes, the danger trees will fall, mushrooms will grow, then fireweed, followed by myriads of other life forms that will repopulate the entire area. In a very short time all will be well again. Demonstrating once again that Nature does not need us, and is probably better off without our presence. So when we, the visitors, do return we must be extra careful to make as little impact as possible, and leave no trace!

As soon as safely possible I will be hiking over the ranges of Cathedral Provincial Park and hopefully farther afield. For two years my worn-out hip joints have slowed me down considerably in hiking around. But now, with two artificial hips, I can continue to experience the wonders of the great outdoors! Renewal is not just for the land.

BIBLIOGRAPHY

Fauna

Burt William.H./Richard P.Grossenheider. *A Field Guide to the Mammals of America North of Mexico*. Peterson Field Guides, 1976.

Duane Sept, J. *Animal Tracks & Signs of the Northwest*. Calypso Publishing, 2012.

Dunn, Jon L. and Jonathan Alderfer. *Field Guide to the Birds of North America*. National Geographic, 2011.

Forest, Louise R. *Field Guide to Tracking Animals in the Snow*. Stackpole Books, 1988.

Flora

Craighead.John .J. *Field Guide to Rocky Mountain Wildflowers*. Peterson Field Guides, 1963.

Parish,Roberta.Ray Coupe, and Dennis Lloyd. *Plants of Southern Interior BC*. Lone Pine Publishing, 1996.

Pojar, Jim and Andy Mackinnon. *Alpine Plants of BC, Alberta, & Northwest North America*. Lone Pine Publishing, 2013.

Geology

Cannings, Sydney, JoAnne Nelson, and Richard Cannings. *Geology of British Columbia*. Greystone Books, 2011.

Mathews, Bill and Jim Monger. *Roadside Geology of Southern British Columbia*. Mountain Press Publishing, 2005.

Maps

Musso Ventures, Ltd. *Backroads Mapbooks: Thompson Okanagan BC* (map 2: Keremeos). Musso Ventures, Ltd.

Site Maps from BC Parks.

Mycology (Mushrooms)

Lincoff, Gary H. *Audubon Society Field Guide to North American Mushrooms.* Alfred A. Knopf, Inc., 1981.

Miller Jr, Orson K. *Mushrooms of North America.* New York: Dutton, 1977.

Trudell, Steve and Joe Ammirati. *Mushrooms of the Pacific North West.* Timber Press, 2009.

GLOSSARY

Alpine meadow. Usually around the treeline in elevation, grassy and flower-filled areas with large spaces between trees.

Anthropocene. The present age, geologically speaking: the age of the presence of mankind.

Basalt. A kind of volcanic rock, essentially cooled lava, usually composed of fine, black crystals.

Benchland. A flat area above an existing or ancient drainage zone that was originally the valley bottom, before post-glacial floods made deeper drainage channels. Composed of glacial deposits.

Berry plants. Used to mean the various plants that produce berries used as a food source by early man. These would include service berries (saskatoons), chokecherries, blueberries, raspberries, strawberries, etc.

Bivvy shelter. Short for "bivouac shelter." An overnight shelter used in emergencies only— for example an overhanging rock or rock shelter,.

Boardwalk. There are many boardwalks in the park. They are wooden pathways to get the hiker safely across marshy sections and creeks, while preserving the environment, to avoid making mudholes in high-traffic areas.

Boulder clay *(see "glacial till").* When glaciers covered the land, the rivers of ice carried rocks, gravel, sand, and silt. When the ice melted, the load was dropped, leaving huge amounts of mixed-up materials of all sizes.

Bushwhack. To go off the trail. In this park, this is often virtually impossible, and very dangerous. There is so much deadfall, and many hidden cliffs.

Buttes. Originally, "buttes" were flat-topped islands of sedimentary rock like those found in the Southwest US; however, though the Twin Buttes were named for this tabletop shape, they are actually volcanic plugs.

Cairn. This is a manmade pile of rocks beside a trail. This signifies that it is not a game trail, and it is easier to follow in snow or misty conditions. Please add a rock when passing a cairn.

Canadian Shield. The original, ancient rock core of North America. The bedrock to the east of the Rockies.

Centennial Trail. This trail was completed in 1967 (Canada's Centennial). It joined together many existing trails to make possible a continuous trail from Manning Park to Chopaka (South of Cawston), with a total distance of eighty-four kilometres.

Cirque, or "cwm" (*Welsh*). A land form created when ice erosion forms a horseshoe-shaped low area below a peak, surrounded, usually, by steep rock slopes.

Clear-cut. The common method of forestry in BC: cut everything, whether or not it is necessary.

Col. A high ridge line between two peaks.

Conglomerate. "Pudding stone"—a solid rock composed of pebbles cemented together by heat and pressure and/or mud or calcium.

Cretaceous. This was the geologic period from 135 to 65 million years ago. The final period of the Mesozoic Era, which finished off the dinosaurs.

Deadfall. Trees that are laying on the ground, either dead from disease or knocked down by the wind, forest fire, landslip, or some other natural phenomenon.

Deciduous. Trees that are deciduous lose their leaves in winter—unlike most conifers, except larch, which loses its needles each winter. Larch trees are therefore both coniferous and deciduous.

Detritus. Loose rock broken off and moved by erosion.

Dewdney Trail. A road construction project to provide a Canadian route to the interior, finished in 1861.

Dykes. A flow of volcanic rock that fills cracks or faults in the bedrock.

Eocene Period. The geological epoch from about 57 to 35 million years ago.

Erosion. The wearing-away of soil and rock by the effects of weather. The changing of the natural surface by the actions of frost, snow, wind, rain, etc.

Fault. A fracture line in rock that has movement and displacement of at least one side of the fracture.

Glacial erratic. A piece of rock that has been carried along by a moving glacier, left in a different location after its melting.

Glacial till. A mixture of rocks, gravel, sand, clay, and silt that was carried along by a moving glacier until it stopped moving and melted, depositing its load.

Glaciation. The formation and movement of ice sheets that covered huge areas of North America at various times, and their recession.

Granite. A type of rock comprised of quartz and feldspar that underlies most of Cathedral Park.

Gravel. Small particles of rock, larger than sand.

Grimface. The mountain that gets the most attention, since it was mentioned in a book of rock scrambles. It should not even be attempted unless you are adequately clothed and prepared. If the weather is damp or windy, a thousand-foot drop awaits the unwary! Be warned.

Grimface Traverse. A technical rock route of 5.6, with some aid needed. The route starts from a col on Mt. Macabre. For rock-climbers only.

Hanging Valley. Originally a stream tributary, where the main valley has been deepened by greater glacial erosion, leaving the tributary valley at a much higher elevation. Usually the hanging valley has a steep drop down to the main valley.

Igneous. A rock type that was originally molten.

International Boundary Survey. Surveys carried out along the 49th Parallel in the late nineteenth century, to mark the United States boundary and incidentally check the geology for any deposits of possible value, such as gold, coal, etc.

Intrusions. The placement of molten rock into an existing rock through cracks and faults.

Jurassic. The geological period before the Cretaceous, from 135 to 190 million years ago.

Kames. The benchlands and hillocks left after a melting glacier has eroded out the original valley bottom.

Kettle Lake. A lake formed from a large block of melting ice left stranded by a retreating glacier.

Landslips. The movement of the land surface downhill. This can be sudden or very slow, depending on materials and slope angle.

Marine fossils. The petrified remains of living organisms that once lived in the ocean.

Metamorphic. Used to describe rock originally below the ground that has been changed by heat and pressure into a different mineral and chemical structure than its original components. For example, limestone can become marble.

Metasequioa. Dawn redwood trees that grew in this area in the Eocene Period.

Miocene. The geological epoch from about 5 to 25 million years ago.

Monolith. A large, upright single piece of stone.

Morraines (*lateral* or *terminal*). The ridges of broken rocks that a melting glacier leaves at the sides or at its end as it melts. As the glacier loses force, it can no longer carry rocky debris.

Muskeg. Swampy, boggy terrain, usually at the valley bottom.

No-trace. An obvious term that few people seem able to adhere to! To leave a place with no evidence of anyone ever having been there.

Octagonal. Eight-sided. Basalt columns form in this way due to the structure of the crystals.

Outfitters' cabins. There have been businesses helping hunters and others to access the backcountry for many years. These businesses often had rustic log cabins to accommodate their clients at the start of the trip. In order to organize all the camping and cooking equipment and the loading of packhorses, they had small corrals at their cabins. Many of these cabins and businesses still exist on the fringes of the park—in Ewart Creek, for example.

Packhorse. The easy way to get all your stuff to the perfect campsite. Even today, packhorse trails are good hiking routes, as the riders carry chainsaws to keep the trails open (outside the park).

Park Facilities Operator. Most of the parks in BC are no longer run by park rangers. The jobs were contracted out years ago to save money. So the person who collects your camping fees, sells the firewood, and cleans the outhouses doesn't necessarily know anything about the actual park!

Patina. The very thin outer coating on a rock due to weathering or staining by foliage. A rock must usually be broken to reveal its true colour.

Patterned ground. Patterns in rock-strewn ground formed by frost action, such as in polygons, net shapes, or circles.

Petrified. Something organic that was turned into stone by the infiltration of mineralized water, like a fossil.

Pine beetle. A rice-grain-sized beetle that bores holes in pine species and lays its eggs. The resulting larvae feed in the under-bark layers and kill the tree before hatching out and flying on to more trees. They are responsible for the huge forest losses in the monocultured pine plantations that we call our forests.

Pine grass (*Calamagrostis rubescens*). The common grass that grows under the pine trees in the drier interior.

Pleistocene. The epoch that lasted about as long as all the ice ages, from about 1.5 million to about 12 thousand years ago.

Pluton. A mass of intrusive granite underground. After erosion and upheavals, they can be visible above ground.

Pyrocumulous. A type of huge cloud that forms above a wildfire. As the fuel burns, gasses, including water vapour and carbon monoxide, rise up thousands of metres and can then create their own weather, with thunder, lightning—even rain, snow, and hail.

Quesnalia. The name given to the rocks that now extend from the Yukon through Quesnel, and to the south of Princeton. They were originally in the ocean, floating on the Earth's crust, and were moved by the tectonic plates into the mainland and pushed relentlessly eastward.

Quiniscoe. He was the chief of the Similkameen Band, and a famed bear hunter. The lake and mountain were named for him after the park was established.

Rockhound. A person who likes to find or collect rocks, for interest or for jewelry.

Sand. Ground-up rock, bigger than silt or clay, but finer than gravel.

Sedges. A large family of grass-like plants that tend to prefer high-altitude, extreme habitats. Difficult-to-identify to species. "Rushes are round, but sedges have edges." You can feel the edges if you twirl them between your fingers.

Sedimentary. Used to describe rock strata that are laid down in layers, such as gravels in riverbeds, or sands under the ocean.

Shuttle. The vehicles that bring guests up the road to the lodge. In high season, there can be vehicles on the road from 8 a.m. until 6 p.m.

Silt. Very fine particles of ground-up rock, coarser than clay.

Skins. These are strips of mohair or similar materials that are glued under skis to enable the user to travel uphill! At the top of a hill, you can remove them and ski down.

Solifluction. A process that can take place in the spring at higher elevations, whereby waterlogged ground can flow slowly downhill over the frozen subsoil at a rate of a few centimetres a year.

Spring runoff. Freshet, resulting in rapid waterflow in all drainages.

Spruce bark beetle. The bug that destroyed 99 percent of the spruce trees at the lodge. Most trees were at least two hundred years old. There are still some small spruce down in the valley. In a natural world, a forest fire would consume them and the tree sequence would begin again.

Tarn. A small, seasonal pond, high on the tundra, usually very shallow.

Tundra. A high-elevation plain with a subarctic climate, covered in sedges, mosses, and alpine flowers. The Rim Trail is mostly on tundra.

Varves. Annual depositions of silt or clay in a shallow pond or lake where there is almost no current. Used to calculate when the last glaciers melted.

Volcanic ash. Fine matter ejected from a volcano that can be powdery or consolidated into tuff or tufa.

Volcanic plug. The cooled lava remaining inside the volcano after an eruption is all that remains, after erosion of the rest of the volcano.

Wildfire. A fire that is freely burning without control. Often, wildfires are started by careless hikers or campers—even hot vehicle exhaust pipes.

Windshell. A garment that is windproof, an essential item if hiking in the park. So much vital body heat is lost without one.

Ypresian. Part of the Eocene Epoch, named after Ypres in Belgium, where this kind of geology exists.

APPENDIX –
Bird Checklist: In Cathedral Park, from the Ashnola Valley to the Rim

- [ ] Common loon
- [ ] Harlequin duck
- [ ] Barrow's goldeneye
- [ ] Ruffed grouse
- [ ] Spruce grouse (Franklin's grouse)
- [ ] White-tailed ptarmigan
- [ ] Sandhill crane
- [ ] Osprey
- [ ] Merlin
- [ ] Sharp-shinned hawk
- [ ] American kestrel
- [ ] Golden eagle
- [ ] Bald eagle
- [ ] Northern pygmy owl
- [ ] Great horned owl
- [ ] Long-eared owl

- [ ] Lesser yellowlegs
- [ ] Vaux's swift
- [ ] Belted kingfisher
- [ ] Clark's nutcracker
- [ ] Common raven
- [ ] Grey jay
- [ ] Hairy woodpecker
- [ ] American three-toed woodpecker
- [ ] Red-naped sapsucker
- [ ] Mountain chickadee
- [ ] White-breasted nuthatch
- [ ] Red-breasted nuthatch
- [ ] Golden-crowned kinglet
- [ ] Ruby-crowned kinglet
- [ ] American dipper
- [ ] Chipping sparrow

- ☐ Dark-eyed junco
- ☐ MacGillivray's warbler
- ☐ Yellow-rumped warbler
- ☐ Townsend's warbler
- ☐ Warbling vireo
- ☐ Swainson's thrush
- ☐ Western tanager
- ☐ Hammond's flycatcher
- ☐ American robin
- ☐ Veery
- ☐ American goldfinch
- ☐ Grey-crowned rosy finch
- ☐ Horned lark
- ☐ White-winged crossbill
- ☐ Red crossbill
- ☐ Cedar waxwing
- ☐ Pine siskin
- ☐ Eastern kingbird
- ☐ Townsend's solitaire

Printed in the USA
CPSIA information can be obtained
at www.ICGtesting.com
JSHW060951081024
71139JS00006B/15